Louis H. Sullivan: *The Banks*

The MIT Press

Cambridge, Massachusetts

London, England

Louis H. Sullivan: *The Banks*

Lauren S. Weingarden

© 1987 by The Massachusetts Institute of Technology

All rights reserved. No part of this book may be reproduced in any form by any electronic or mechanical means (including photocopying, recording, or information storage and retrieval) without permission in writing from the publisher.

This book was set in Helvetica and Galliard by Achorn Graphic Services and printed and bound by Murray Printing Company in the United States of America.

Library of Congress Cataloging-in-Publication Data

Weingarden, Lauren S., 1948–
Louis H. Sullivan: the banks, 1906–1920.

Bibliography: p.

1. Sullivan, Louis H., 1856–1924—Criticism and interpretation. 2. Architecture, Modern—20th century—Middle West. 3. Prairie School (Architecture).
4. Banks and banking—Middle West. I. Title.
NA712.5.P73W45 1987   725′.24′0924   87-2729
ISBN 0-262-23130-1

Published with the assistance of the J. Paul Getty Trust

In loving memory of my mother Shirley Davidson

Contents

A Historical Survey

Color Plates   32

A Catalogue of the Banks

Foreword

No matter how much scholarship is devoted to the figure of Louis Sullivan, the enigma of his life and work seems inexhaustible. Metropolitan demiurge and Celtic mystic, Chicago patrician and midwestern democrat, transcendentalist and realist, Sullivan stalks through the *fin de siècle* American landscape like a Titanic ghost. The myth of his alcoholism, his neurasthenia and bohemian behavior, above all, perhaps, his painful worldly failure after the dissolution of his partnership with Adler—all these have served to prejudice his achievement and cloud his reputation. There is something Greek about his meteoric rise and fall, as there is something tragic about the brilliant flowering and brief duration of the Prairie School, even if the facts testify to a span of activity that extends beyond Sullivan's demise in 1924. And yet despite this, the power of Sullivan's architecture remains. Indeed, one may claim that his reputation and influence are all set to grow rather than diminish, so that the hitherto indifferently regarded rural banks of his late career are now to be seen as the rich apotheosis of his total output. As this study demonstrates, the current reappraisal is due in large measure to the painstaking research of scholars like Lauren Weingarden, to her discovery of the invaluable Henry Fuermann photo archive, as well as to the magnificent colored photographs of the extant banks taken by the architect Crombie Taylor.

Apart from providing a detailed evaluation of each of the eight rural banks that Sullivan designed between 1906 and 1920—a study given an unusual historical depth through citations from contemporary critical appraisals of the works—the author also broadens our understanding of Sullivan's intentions in relation to the emerging midwestern culture of his time. Convincingly enough, Weingarden sees this last as an expression of economic and spiritual independence on the part of a prosperous rural hinterland which at the turn of the century attempted to liberate itself from the material and cultural domination of the all-powerful Chicago. For this purpose it chose to back the waning Prairie School rather than to follow the Beaux-Arts classicism that Chicago had embraced after its popular triumph at the World's Fair of 1893.

Leonardo Benevolo, among others, has shown us that the so-called betrayal of the Prairie School was inevitable, given the rapacity of American expansion at the turn of the century. And yet, however unavoidable this may have been, we are left with the impression that the ensuing cultural conformity had a negative impact on the evolution of American architecture as a whole. With the exception of Wright, Elmslie, and Bennet, and their respective apprentices, all Sullivanians to a man, the Prairie School was to have little issue of consequence in the second quarter of our century. Thus Sullivan's banks may be seen, along with the Prairie School, which ended definitively with Wright's death, as the swan song of a culture that somehow never fully matured. The current resurgence of interest in Prairie School architecture seems timely because it offers another point of departure for the "historicism" of the postmodern era, one that just might be able to steer between the dead-end of a pseudo-classical revival and the tiresome permutations of a reductive eclecticism.

Far from resorting to eclecticism, Sullivan had in mind a recourse to Nature as the only available bedrock of value in a secular age, an age that was bereft of any belief, apart from the treadmill of pursuing material wealth as an end in itself. In this respect it is surprising to discover that, like the little-known regional school of midwestern structural artists who were to follow him much later, such as the constructionist Charles Biederman, Sullivan sought to create a chromatic tectonic tone poem about that intersection between Nature and Culture that he envisaged as being embodied in all genuine works of architecture. The rural banks, far from being marginal, were essential to the fulfillment of this vision since they afforded the presence of a public institution, a type form that was hardly available in the abstract, repetitious, rental floors of Sullivan's high-rise structures. This may well explain why the banks, like Wright's Larkin Building of 1904, were conceived as surrogate churches, complete with side aisles and a nave culminating at the end of the central axis in the altar of the glistening vault, deliberately exposed as the symbol of private and communal wealth. Sullivan's naive idealism in this regard was surely a good deal more justified than the limitless skepticism which today serves us so badly in answering the practical demands of our time.

What is perhaps of greatest significance for us is the multiple levels on which Sullivan's tectonic tone poems were designed to work, for while they embodied all the functional advantages of modern technology in the service of the democratic banking hall (I have in mind Sullivan's pioneering use of the steel frame, plate glass, electroplating, built-in central heating, and advanced systems of plenum ventilation), they also served as elaborate light modulators, not only of their own intrinsic radiance, but more importantly of the changing ambient light. This light was subject not only to seasonal and diurnal cycles, but also to the peculiar chromatic luminosity of the surrounding landscape. Herein Sullivan was to happen on an almost limitless expressivity and one that has been sorely neglected of late. He realized, as few have since, that the fabric and the volume of any given structure possess a luminous potential of equal power to the contextual environment in which it happens to be situated. He saw that the building and the site, when sensitively inter-

related, have the capacity to form a new and resonantly vital whole. This is surely the still-valid legacy of the contrasting chromatic "pointillism," directly derived from Chevreul and the Impressionists. This tessellated chromaticism runs throughout the fabric of these astonishing works, as the eye passes from multi-hued and tinted textual brickwork to encrusted terra cotta facing, or from the fashionable Craftsman's green of the stained oak to the blue-green stenciled, decorative, oriental iterations on the surface of the receding reveals as they rise high and wide, within the span, above the green marble revetment and the electroplated chandeliers of the space below. Last but not least, we should not overlook the metallic highlights of the teller's grills and the multiple impact of the stained and tinted glass, which is an ever-present source of iridescent light.

Something of German Romantic Classicism also lies beneath this synaesthesia, which could have degenerated into mere polychromatic appearances had it not been for the tectonic tessellation of the pigmented surfaces. Sullivan's delicate, not to say ineffable, approach is probably indebted, in some degree, to the German architectural theorist Gottfried Semper, whose influence on the Prairie School is well known, even if the extent of its impact in this instance is difficult to assess. We may surely look to Semper, however, for the idea of the brick wall as a petrified textile screen, just as we have to credit him with the notion of a functionalism that went beyond utilitarianism, thereby allowing for form to be inflected by such factors as material substance, production method, climate, light, landfall, and even more arcane regional considerations. This dichotomous Semperian legacy is suggested by Sullivan's use of tinted pressed brick, the texture being a device with which to offset the "mechanical, intellectual activities'' of architectural design, thereby avoiding, as Weingarden points out, the reduction of architecture to nothing but an expression of facts.

Sullivan's rural banks are comprised of pressed and wire-cut bricks that seem to glow with an inner radiance as one approaches them. At the time they assumed the appearance of elaborate jewel cases within the midst of the rather undistinguished midwestern towns. That this was a conscious intent on Sullivan's part is borne out by the following remarkable passage. He wrote of his beloved textured brick: "Manufacturers by grinding the clay of the shale coarse and by use of cutting wires, produced on its face a new and most interesting texture, a texture with a nap-like effect, suggesting somewhat an Anatolian rug; a texture giving innumerable highlights and shadows, and a moss-like softness of appearance.''

Surely no brick masonry was ever more woven in its generic conception than this. At the same time, the allusion to Anatolian textiles returns us to the perennial obsession of Sullivan's mature career, namely, his orientalism, with which he hoped to create an independent tectonic culture for the New World, one which, while totally surpassing European eclecticism, the inane "battle of styles," would also be capable of engendering an unprecedented democratic architecture, comparable to the glories of Islam and to the lost splendor of Egypt and Mesopotamia.

Richardson, Sullivan, and Wright practiced at a time when America, despite the dark shadow of genocide, still possessed the utopian promise of a new frontier. They were the architects of a seemingly golden century when, for all the rapacities of capitalism, America still seemed to be on the brink of realizing an unprecedented secular order—an order that was egalitarian by constitutional definition, a promised land of apparently infinite wealth wherein the machine in the garden had yet to reveal its potential capacity for destroying the entire world. Even in Wright's Oak Park period, which coincided, around the time of the First World War, with the last creative period of Sullivan's career, commodified building had yet to scatter its detritus over the land, and the public realm, the very touchstone of architecture, was not so diminished as it is now by the combined forces of media and mobility. For Sullivan and Wright alike there still remained the promise of an organic architecture which, through the agency of a natural democracy, would eventually prove itself capable of reconciling, for the first time in human history, the age-old conflict between Nature and Culture. This promise of being able to live in harmony with a natural benevolence—wherein, as the Enlightenment had envisaged, Nature herself would become the ultimate deity— was undermined by the advent of the Depression and by the concomitant disasters of the First and Second World Wars. It is this surely which gives Sullivan's rural banks their peculiar poignancy, for the local agrarian wealth which they once so proudly represented was to be less readily assured, and the local capital which once depended on regional generation and on a regular cycle of investment and measured growth tended to be increasingly dispersed in various forms of global development, which led to the abstract indifference of international monopoly.

Sullivan already foresaw this fate when he wrote of the demise of the Prairie School after the Columbia Exposition of 1893: "The flag was in the breeze. Then there appeared two clouds on the horizon. The first of these was 1893 and the second was called Baring Brothers.'' If Sullivan's banks are still capable of speaking to us in terms other than their brilliant aestheticism, then they may well serve to remind us of the fact that the only way to sustain a profound architectural culture is through some measure of regional cultivation.

Kenneth Frampton

Acknowledgments

This study represents one part of my investigations into Louis H. Sullivan's theory and practice. I began this body of work as a graduate student under the guidance of Richard Shiff, who, as both friend and mentor, has been a constant source of intellectual inspiration and personal support. During the production of this book many other scholars and institutional administrators have generously shared their time and expertise with me. Here, however, I can acknowledge only those with whom I worked most closely.

Kenneth Frampton and Patricia Rose read earlier versions of the manuscript; from their helpful comments and suggestions I greatly benefited. Each was more than generous in helping me obtain monetary support for the publication of this book. I am also thankful to Chris Otto, who in many ways has sustained an enthusiasm for my work on Sullivan; on many occasions his collegial support has been a tremendous incentive. Alys Palladino-Craig, Director of the Fine Arts Gallery at The Florida State University, facilitated a photographic exhibition of Sullivan's banks that I curated in the fall of 1984. That event allowed me to preview what this monograph was to be: an occasion to re-view Sullivan's bank designs as multifaceted variations of a single conceptual and chromatic theme.

Crombie Taylor spent many hours with me discussing the banks and describing them in loving detail. Over the years he has been a judicious and enthusiastic renovator, conservator, and archivist of Sullivan's works. Many Sullivan scholars have benefited directly and indirectly from his work, but I personally gained a wealth of insight from his lucid yet lyrical architectural perceptions. Jeffrey Plank initiated the original collaboration between Crombie and me. I am thankful to him for his pre-vision and for sharing with me his editorial skills and critical inquiries during this book's production.

John Zukowsky, Curator of Architecture at The Art Institute of Chicago, and Mary Woolever, Architectural Librarian and Archivist, provided kind and expeditious assistance in locating documents and reproducing drawings and photographs from the Sullivan archives. Janet Parks, Curator of Drawings at the Avery Architectural Library of Columbia University, and her staff were also prompt and resourceful in assisting me with viewing and reproducing Sullivan drawings in the Avery collection. While Chester Brummel's expert photography enhanced my earlier scholarship on Sullivan, his enduring friendship helped me gain access to many of the vintage photographs reproduced in the present work. David Phillips kindly accommodated my various needs by expertly reproducing the Henry Fuermann photographs.

I also want to thank Paul Sprague, who shared with me important archival material from his seminal work on Sullivan. As a Sullivan scholar I am most indebted to Sprague's scholarship; he was the first historian to demonstrate that Sullivan was a master draftsman and designer of ornament. Timothy Samuelson and John Vinci, two other preeminent Sullivan scholars, were also generous in giving me access to their photographic documents.

When I visited the banks during the spring and summer of 1984, many bank officers and administrators kindly shared their recollections of the bank buildings' histories and gave me access to archival collections. I was also generously assisted in my research by the staffs of local historical societies and libraries. To each individual, I owe many thanks. I am particularly grateful to Ferdinand Freytag, preservationist-architect of the

Peoples Savings and Loan Association in Sidney, Ohio. He personally took me on a tour of the Sidney bank and its surrounding buildings. With his guidance I gained a new appreciation of Sullivan's technological and functionalist solutions. Equally important, Mr. Freytag not only facilitated my work in the bank's archives, but also loaned me materials from his personal archival collection.

I deeply appreciate the professional guidance and encouragement of Carter Manny, Director of the Graham Foundation for Advanced Studies in the Fine Arts, and of Deborah Marrow, Assistant Director of the Getty Grant Program. In 1983 I received a grant from the Graham Foundation to begin the research for this project. More recently, the Getty Trust provided a subvention that made it possible to include color reproductions in the completed volume. I also wish to express my deep gratitude to the staff of The MIT Press, especially to three people who helped me keep faith during the final stages of production. To Roger Conover for his unrelenting energy in and commitment to bringing this work to its completed form; to Debbi Edelstein for her good sense and good humor in closely attending to detail; and to Diane Jaroch for her many talents in closing the last, but not least important, gap(s) to make this work whole.

Finally, I shall always be grateful to my friends, who gave freely their invaluable support, advice, and compassion during the various stages of this project. And to my family, who may still question, but never undermine, my determination to shed new light on lost meanings in Sullivan's works. I thank them for understanding and for being there.

Introduction

Between 1906 and 1920 Louis H. Sullivan designed and built eight rural town banks in Minnesota, Iowa, Indiana, Ohio, and Wisconsin. These banks count among the few commissions Sullivan received from 1895 until his death in 1924, yet they rank with his finest designs. Modestly scaled, but monumentally conceived, the banks constitute a new phase in Sullivan's ongoing refinement of the forms and theories he first realized in his skyscrapers. Sullivan is best known for this earlier achievement. During his partnership with Dankmar Adler (1881–95), he became a leading designer of urban commercial building types, especially the steel-frame skyscraper. Like his skyscraper designs, the rural banks bear witness to Sullivan's enduring search for a new American style, a search that secured him a place among the innovators of modern architecture.

Most modernist historians and critics who admired Sullivan's skyscrapers viewed the banks as Sullivan's "late works." They treated them negatively and unevenly and as the swan song to his career. We can now reassess the banks by separating two interrelated ways they have traditionally been viewed. These views often resulted in the modernists' misgivings about Sullivan's designs. The first is a historical one: modernist historians and critics equated architectural excellence with the straightforward representation of construction, material, and use. They grounded their formal analyses in technological and programmatic determinism, the tenets of twentieth-century functionalist design methods. While modernist observers correctly discerned elements of functionalist design in Sullivan's architectural compositions, they overemphasized the primacy of these solutions in Sullivan's own procedures.

The second obstacle to a fuller appreciation of the banks resides in the black-and-white photographs by which they have been judged. With the first monograph published on Sullivan's complete works, Hugh Morrison's *Louis Sullivan: Prophet of Modern Architecture* (1935), black-and-white photographs became the standard documents for modernist formal analysis. Morrison, who praised Sullivan's color harmonies in the banks, warned against evaluating the banks with these photographs alone (p. 208; see Bibliography at the back of this volume). But the monochromatic images reinforced modernist critical biases by presenting the buildings in isolation and with tonal contrasts that exaggerated those features which were either consistent or inconsistent with twentieth-century functionalist values.

The purpose of this monograph is to restore the original integrity of Sullivan's designs for rural town banks. To this end, I have limited my study to a network of architectural and extra-architectural issues that Sullivan addressed in solving the problems of this particular building type. I have determined such issues by their recurrence in Sullivan's written and visual statements and by the critical discourse that surrounded these statements. It is not my purpose here to discuss another set of historiographic problems regarding "influences" generated between Sullivan and his Prairie School followers or between Sullivan and other turn-of-the-century bank designers. Nevertheless, throughout this study I maintain a historical perspective related to these broader questions. That is, I view Sullivan's artistic behavior as partly conditioned by a visual critical dialogue with his "followers," especially his former chief draftsmen Frank Lloyd Wright (1888–93) and George Grant Elmslie (1893–1909), and with the community of American architects at large.[1] More pertinent to this study is my contention that while the banks show Sullivan to have shared certain tendencies with his progressive and more conservative colleagues, these tendencies were also present in his own earlier works. Both the kind of commission for rural town banks and the method of his critical discourse enabled Sullivan to rehearse, refine, and clarify a variety of formal and technical features in these "late works" that he had previously devised for other building types.

While aspects of Sullivan's development and achievements in relation to his contemporaries merit scholarly attention in their own right, I believe a reappraisal of his banks can also provide a better understanding of his historical place within nineteenth- and twentieth-century American cultural, artistic, and architectural traditions. I proceed with such a reappraisal in two ways. First, in "A Historical Survey," I review the banks as a group. In topic-oriented sections I discuss aspects of Sullivan's solutions to the rural bank as a specific building type and as consonant with his search for a new style. I also use the observations of Sullivan's contemporary critics as starting points for recounting his original problems and solutions and the degree to which he satisfied critical standards of his time. Montgomery Schuyler, A. N. Rebori, and Thomas Tallmadge provide firsthand descriptions and comparative analyses of the banks as well as personal interviews with Sullivan. Each of these critics observed the functional aspects of the buildings. More importantly, they paid close attention to parts of Sullivan's designs that have been neglected by most modernist viewers. Foremost among these latter features are architectural and decorative polychromy; the formal unity of ornament, mass, and structural elements; the contextual relationship between the banks and their settings; and the "democratic" meanings Sullivan attributed to his functionalist layouts.

In "A Catalogue of the Banks," I follow a second method of investiga-tion. I treat the banks separately in order to reconstruct the conditions of each commission, the building history of each project, and Sullivan's compositional methods. To this end, I make more direct use of raw data obtained from bank archives, reports from local newspapers, and local historical studies. Most of the banks have been subject to physical changes ranging from radical remodeling to adaptive renovations. I therefore attempt to give detailed descriptions of the original appearance of each bank by combining early twentieth-century written documents with primary visual documents—vintage photographs taken upon the completion of each bank, preliminary sketches, working drawings, and color photographs of a more recent date.

I would like to note briefly that many of the vintage photographs in this volume have been selected from original glass-plate negatives produced by Henry Fuermann, a photographer for the Chicago Architectural Photographing Company. (Now defunct, this company's extant negatives are presently maintained as an archival collection by David R. Phillips.) Fuermann, a Chicago colleague and friend of Sullivan, spent several days photographing each bank immediately before occupancy. I reproduce Fuermann's photographs uncropped since these views often provide contextual references to Sullivan's design solutions.

Note

1.

In particular, present-day scholars have
compared Sullivan's banks with Frank
Lloyd Wright's project for a Village Bank
(1901) and the City National Bank (Mason
City, Iowa; 1909–10) and with George
Grant Elmslie's and William Gray Purcell's
(who also had worked for Sullivan in 1907)
Merchant's Bank of Winona (Winona, Min-
nesota; 1911–12) and the Farmers and
Merchants Bank of Hector (Hector, Minnesota; 1917). See Kenneth W. Severens,
"The Reunion of Louis Sullivan and Frank
Lloyd Wright," *The Prairie School Review*
12 (Third Quarter 1975): 5–22; David
Gebhard, "Louis Sullivan and George
Grant Elmslie," *Journal of the Society of
Architectural Historians* 19 (May 1960): 66–
68; H. Allen Brooks, *The Prairie School:
Frank Lloyd Wright and his Midwest Contemporaries* (Toronto: University of Toronto Press, 1972), pp. 202–5, 300–2. For a
contemporary view of Sullivan in comparison with other early twentieth-century bank
designers, see "Recent Bank Buildings of
the United States," *Architectural Record*
25 (January 1909): 1–55.

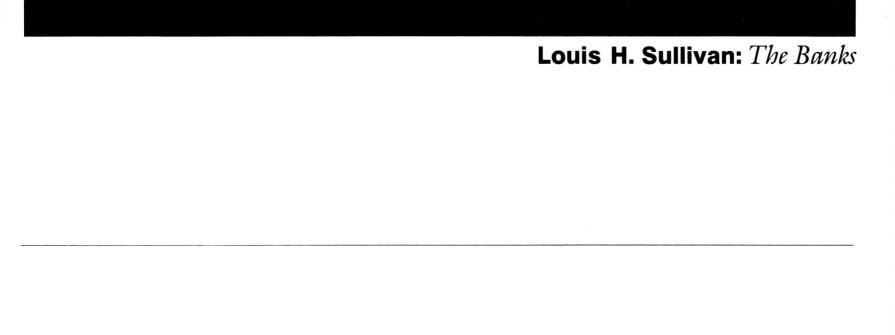

Louis H. Sullivan: *The Banks*

The Critical Legacy of the Banks

Contemporary critics ranked the banks with Sullivan's most successful designs for skyscrapers, especially the Wainwright Building (1890) and the Guaranty Building (1894–95). These critics recognized the rural bank as a new building type shaped by a new set of programmatic, technological, and historical conditions. They praised Sullivan for extending his mature artistic skills and technical excellence to this new architectural problem. Upon the completion of the first bank, the National Farmers' Bank in Owatonna, Minnesota (1906–8), an anonymous writer for the *Architectural Record* noted that it "point[ed] a new direction in architectural thought" (figures 6–11).[1] This reviewer identified Sullivan's achievements by making two important observations that persisted in the popular and professional accounts of Sullivan's bank designs. He praised the formal unity between functional and artistic features and the overall harmony between the bank building and the townscape.

Montgomery Schuyler, A. N. Rebori, and Thomas Tallmadge count among the foremost critics of early twentieth-century progressive architecture. They developed the earliest criteria for evaluating Sullivan's banks with the critical standards derived from his skyscraper designs. They continued to admire in the banks Sullivan's mastery of an organic design process for satisfying both functionalist and decorative exigencies. But for these later works they reviewed more thoroughly Sullivan's integration of a straightforward articulation of the plan with the varied nuances of polychromy and ornamentation. Furthermore, these critics interpreted Sullivan's solutions to practical and social needs as "democratic" and as a sign of his enduring leadership in formulating a new American style.

In "The Architecture of Democracy" (1916) Rebori reviewed three of

Sullivan's banks: the Merchants National Bank in Grinnell, Iowa (1913–14) (figures 5, 32); the Home Building Association Bank in Newark, Ohio (1914) (figures 39, 44); and the Land and Loan Office in Algona, Iowa (1913) (figure 25).[2] This review is paradigmatic: it shows how Sullivan's contemporaries combined standards for "organic" functionalism, artistic refinement, and democratic social behavior to interpret Sullivan's architectural achievements.

Rebori began his review with a discussion of the preliminary sketches Sullivan made at the site of the Grinnell bank (figures 1–3). He used these documents to describe Sullivan's organic process of design:

Sullivan arrives at a solution of a given problem by means of a carefully worked out plan in which the allotted areas arranged as to need dominate the treatment, and the outward appearance of the building is permitted to develop accordingly, with the method of construction taking form naturally.[3]

Rebori believed, as did Sullivan, that functional representation must be artistically refined so as to become architecture. He added:

But as all structural conditions are not pleasing to the eye or worthy to be classed as architecture, his artistic instinct causes him to add decoration or adjust proportions, as the case may be, obtaining a justness and balance that is both structural and beautiful.[4]

Rebori concluded this passage by connecting Sullivan's artistic individuality to a specifically American historical and cultural milieu. That is, he saw Sullivan's organic and personal solutions to practical and artistic problems as the products of "the true spirit of democracy":

Sullivan at least stands in a class by himself, for indeed his architecture is not one of imitation, but an architecture that gives a truthful and idealistic modern interpretation of a given problem in a most intimate and individualistic way. It is the true spirit of democracy, expressed in terms of building, significant of our times, our people, and our life. I believe it to be this and more, by virtue of the skill displayed by the designer in the artistic spacing of his decoration, and in the placing and scale of the detail, and in the study given the design as a whole based on function, logic, and art.[5]

As Rebori made clear, Sullivan's ability to fuse functional, structural, and artistic solutions for the rural banks established his preeminence in advanced American architecture. But Sullivan's artistic procedures were informed by his more extensive concerns about the relationships between art, technology, and nature.

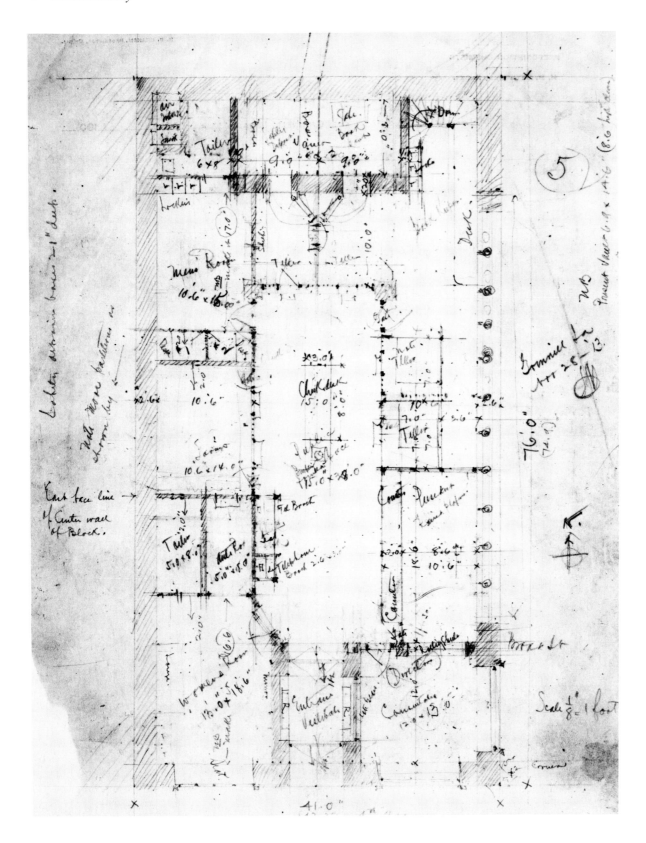

1
Merchants National Bank, Grinnell, Iowa, 1913–15. Preliminary drawing of main floor plan, 28 November 1913. Pencil on paper. Michigan Historical Collections, Bentley Historical Library, The University of Michigan.

2
Merchants National Bank, preliminary drawing of main elevation, 30 November 1913. Pencil on paper. Michigan Historical Collections, Bentley Historical Library, The University of Michigan.

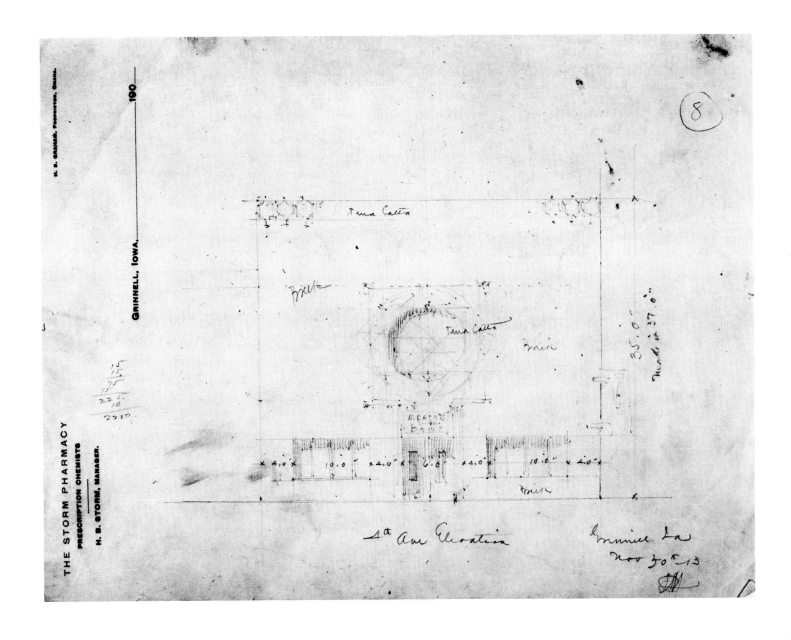

3
**Merchants National Bank, preliminary
drawing of east elevation, 30 November
1913. Pencil on paper. Michigan Historical
Collections, Bentley Historical Library,
The University of Michigan.**

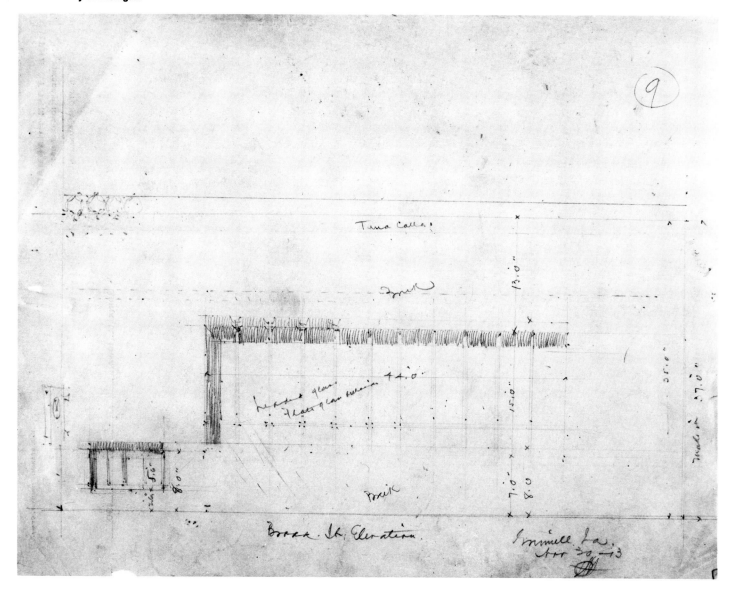

Making the Ideal Real: Sullivan's Theory and Practice

While Sullivan's defenders identified the progressive architectural and social ramifications of his individual style, many missed the strategies Sullivan used to communicate the metaphysical meanings he attached to his architectural compositions.[6] In fact, the majority of his sympathizers were not aware of what Sullivan regarded as the essence of artistic creation.[7] Sullivan designed architecture to articulate, with abstract tectonic (that is, structural) forms and naturalistic decorative schemes, a nineteenth-century transcendentalist discourse.

Throughout his career, Sullivan sought to use architectural elements as symbols for metaphysical truths derived from nature. He inherited this symbol-making project from Walt Whitman, who, in turn, had extended Ralph Waldo Emerson's transcendentalist concepts and procedures. Sullivan's predecessors envisioned a transcendental democracy in which each individual is free to attain spiritual insights as a precondition for physical and moral well-being. Within this system, they assigned to the poet and visual artist the social task of averting an imbalance between material gains and spiritual growth. Specifically, Emerson predicted that an indigenous art form would result when the mechanical and utilitarian arts were united with the fine arts. To this end, Emerson instructed innovators in every medium to decipher the symbolic forms of nature, to show, in turn, the divine cause of all human production. He thus claimed, "Nature offers all her creatures as a picture-language, as symbols, because nature is a symbol in the whole and in every part."[8]

Following these transcendentalist methods, Sullivan provided rational solutions to the practical and technological problems of the building program, but he did not regard these solutions as ends in themselves. Rather, in the skyscrapers and in the banks that followed, he used reductivist structural elements and simple geometric masses as his points of departure for making architecture philosophical.

In his theoretical writings Sullivan explained how he devised an original mode of "organic" ornament through a synthesis of visual and conceptual opposites. He combined botanical and geometric motifs as a "poetic" or "subjective" means for relieving the "mechanical" or "objective" parts of architecture.[9] Two sketches for the Peoples Savings and Loan Association in Sidney, Ohio (1916–18) illustrate the combinatory and symbol-making procedures that Sullivan first realized for his ornamental designs. His drawing for a relief exemplifies (figure 4) how he composed his "organic" ornament with seed-pod and leaf imagery unified by spiraling, undulating, and curvilinear forms. His preliminary sketch for the main elevation (figure 47) illustrates how he reduced the elements of architecture to simple, abstract geometric shapes of half-circles, squares, and rectangles. As the final work shows, whether Sullivan had his ornamental designs executed in plaster, terra cotta, mosaics, wood, or metal, he designed and arranged his ornament so as to dissolve inert surfaces and enliven rigid contours (figure 46; plates 10–12).

With these procedures for producing an organic-subjective and an inorganic-objective means of representation, Sullivan attempted to provide a visual metaphor for what he called the "Infinite Creative Spirit." Sullivan described the Infinite Creative Spirit as a dynamic cosmic force. It both generates and synthesizes subjective and objective phenomena. Pervading both humanity and nature, the Infinite Creative Spirit joins all human endeavors with timeless, organic processes.

Sullivan most cogently stated this dialectic philosophical idea and its consequences for art in his 1894 essay "Emotional Architecture as Com-

4
Peoples Savings and Loan Association,
Sidney, Ohio, 1916–18. Drawing for relief
ornament, "plaster band in wood frieze,"
3 October 1917. Pencil on paper. Collec-
tion of Marilyn and Wilbert R. Hasbrouck,
FAIA.

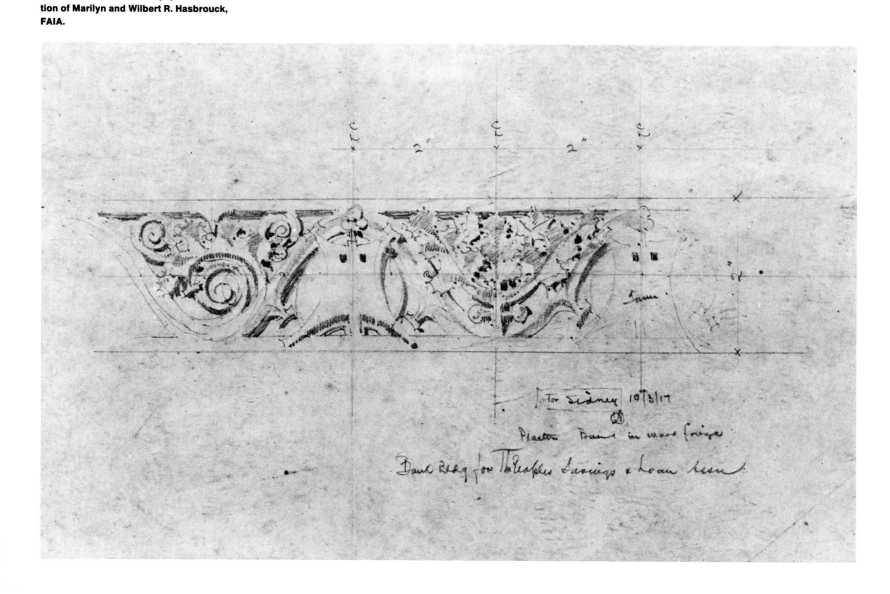

pared with Intellectual: A Study of Objective and Subjective." Here he explained that the creative process of the artist must follow the creative process of nature since the origin of all true art resides in nature. He claimed that as in nature, *"it is the presence of this unreality* [the Infinite Creative Spirit] *that makes the work of art real: it is by virtue of this silent subjectivity that the objective voice of an art song becomes sonorous and thrilling"* (original emphasis).[10]

Sullivan formulated his well-known credo "form follows function" on the basis of these dialectical processes. He first postulated "form follows function" in "The Tall Office Building Artistically Considered" (1896), where he conceived it as the organic design process for the skyscraper and he defined its dual meanings. Sullivan began his essay by using a nineteenth-century rationalist argument to explain that this natural "law" determines the straightforward, practical solutions for planning and constructing the skyscraper. But more importantly, Sullivan defined "form follows function" as a "philosophical observation."[11] With such a view, he made the rational design process analogous with nature's process. Sullivan thus identified "form follows function" as the means for showing the spiritual unity underlying surface appearances—"the flow of life . . . the essence of things [unceasingly] taking shape in the matter of things."[12]

In *Kindergarten Chats* (1901–2) Sullivan allowed his architectural student, whom he was reeducating in nature, to restate the philosophical meaning of "form follows function" in more conventional terms:

The gist of [it] is, I take it, behind every form we see there is a vital something or other which we do not see, yet which makes itself visible to us in that very form. In other words, in a state of nature the form exists *be-cause* of the function, and this something behind the form is neither more nor less than a manifestation of what you call the infinite creative spirit, and what I call God.

The student concluded:

Just as every form contains its function, and exists by virtue of it, so every function finds or is engaged in finding its form. And, furthermore, . . . this is true of the every-day things we see about us in nature and in the reflection of nature we call human life . . . because it is a universal law, of everything that the human mind can take hold of.[13]

We can retrieve Sullivan's symbol-making techniques by rejoining these philosophical statements with their analogous visual forms. Sullivan used "form follows function" as a conceptual guide for submitting the facts of tectonic realism to the symbols or organic idealism. He followed this strategy to make each building an occasion for the spectator/user to transcend the restrictions of physical existence and to enter a spiritual communion with nature and the forces that shaped it.

It is perhaps ironic that Sullivan more fully realized his symbol-making program in the banks than in the skyscrapers. The actual magnitude of the skyscraper and its multiple uses—banks, stores, rental office space, and sometimes, even, theaters—precluded encountering the parts as dynamically integrated with the whole. With the smaller dimensions and more limited functions of the banks, Sullivan attained a more continuous cognitive experience between the exterior and interior. He created such an aesthetic event by enriching his artistic techniques: he composed naturalistic color schemes to envelop logically conceived layouts and elevations.

Polychromy and the Colors of Nature

Thomas Tallmadge believed Sullivan's use of polychromy was among his most significant contributions to the formation of a modern American architecture. Considering this contribution, Tallmadge could view with nearly perfect historical hindsight the place of the banks (and especially what would be Sullivan's last bank[14]) within the context of Sullivan's earlier works. He had personally witnessed Sullivan's accomplishment in rendering the brilliant, polychromatic exterior of the Transportation Building at the 1893 Chicago World's Fair. Therefore, when he reviewed the Farmers and Merchants Union Bank in Columbus, Wisconsin (1919–20; figures 59, 60, 63, 64; plate 14), Tallmadge aligned Sullivan's earlier artistic achievement with his most recent one. "Mr. Sullivan's genius rises to the opportunities as fresh and brilliant as we beheld him thirty years ago in the rainbow arches of the Transportation Building."[15] Here, as in his reviews of the other banks, Tallmadge emphasized Sullivan's transformation of ordinary building materials into sumptuous, polychromatic "jewel"-like apparitions that illuminated the lessons of democracy.

Tallmadge contended that a new American architecture would take place in native rural America. Conversely, he argued that artificial tastes for classical revival styles stifled an artistic rebirth in urban America. In view of these contrasts, he observed that in his rural banks Sullivan was free to realize more fully his artistic ideals and to advance a modern American style. Tallmadge explained that Sullivan contributed to "the artistic development of our non-urban population" by introducing "color, brilliance, and gaiety" into the rural townscape. He further maintained that Sullivan's chromatic "palette" of "concrete, brick, terra cotta and steel, glass mosaics, marble, plaster and wood" completed the social and didactic functions of a new architecture shaped by modern uses, conveniences, and inventions. Tallmadge emphasized Sullivan's achievements by contrasting the banks with "the thin, awkward and wan examples of the country builder, [and with] the pallid and pudgy Roman frontispieces of the city architect."[16]

Sullivan's skillful mixing of the materials of his "palette" and Tallmadge's descriptions of their chromatic effects established a tradition in which local residents nicknamed the banks "jewel boxes" (plates 1, 5, 10, 11). Indeed, when one approaches the banks from any direction, they seem to glow with an inner radiance. Sullivan achieved these radiant nuances by using chromatically "tinted" pressed brick as a facing material for all but one of the bank exteriors.

Writing in 1910, Sullivan explained why he introduced in the banks this newly developed medium of pressed brick.[17] He first discussed how he used it as clay: like this plastic modeling material, pressed brick allowed "the full expression of the plan" so that the whole exterior could be read simply and clearly as "the natural and appropriate forms . . . evidencing, instead of hiding, the working conditions of the building [and] its individuality." Sullivan regarded this straightforward representation of internal conditions the simplest and most commonplace use of the new brick. He claimed that its full advantages could only be realized through the "artistic" treatment of these reductivist masses. In other words, Sullivan used tinted pressed brick to offset the "mechanical," "intellectual activities" of architectural design, so as to avoid treating architecture as "simply an expression of facts."[18]

Sullivan thus examined the artistic benefits of tinted pressed brick for creating a naturalistic architectural representation. He favored rough-cut, tinted pressed brick because with it he could recreate the transitory effects of natural lights and shadows. He suggested these effects when he explained:

Manufacturers by grinding the clay or shale coarse and by the use of cutting wires, produced on its face a new and most interesting texture, a texture with a nap-like effect, suggesting somewhat an Anatolian rug; a texture giving innumerable highlights and shadows, and a moss-like softness of appearance.[19]

What seems like an incongruous analogy between textiles and nature actually can be understood in terms of Sullivan's familiarity with popular nineteenth-century treatises on color theory.[20] This is especially so regarding Michel Eugène Chevreul's *Law of Simultaneous Contrast of Colors* (1839), an edition of which Sullivan owned.[21]

Sullivan's knowledge of Chevreul's treatise and, possibly, of Ogden N. Rood's *Student's Textbook of Modern Chromatics* (1879) provides a basis for comparing Sullivan's procedures as a colorist with those of Impressionist and Neo-Impressionist painters. It is well known that these painters, such as Claude Monet and Georges Seurat, developed from Chevreul's and Rood's treatises their techniques for the optical blending of contrasting and analogous hues as a means of reproducing the diaphonous effects of changing atmospheric light in nature.[22] Chevreul, who drew on his experience as director of dyes at the Gobelin tapestry works from 1824 to 1852, formulated the "law of simultaneous contrast of colors" to enable painters and decorators to attain greater chromatic intensity than could be obtained with the physical mixture of pigments. He prescribed how to juxtapose pure pigments so that optical blending and chromatic enrichment occurs when the pigments are viewed simultaneously. Rood later revised this law with more concrete scientific data

and with more specific instructions for the landscape painter. He argued that uniformly broken pigments applied to the canvas according to the law of simultaneous contrast of colors best approximate the overall luminosity, transience, and transparency of sunlight. Rood also emphasized this technique as the means for depicting the altered chromatic nuances produced by changing cycles of days and seasons.

Sullivan alluded to his own Impressionist or Neo-Impressionist techniques for tinted brick when he grounded his artistic methods for attaining naturalistic effects in the law of simultaneous contrast of colors. He thus rehearsed Chevreul's and Rood's quasi-scientific discourse in describing the optical effects produced by contrasting brick hues, ranging from yellows, oranges, and reds through violets and blues, on a broad, flat surface:

When [tinted bricks] are laid up promiscuously, especially if the surface is large, and care is taken to avoid patches of any one color, the general tone suggests that of a very old oriental rug, and the differing color values of the individual bricks, however sharply these may seem to contrast at close view, are taken up and harmonized in the prevailing general tone. Comprised of many colors, this general tone is, in a sense, neutral and is rich and impressive.[23]

The original intensity of these hues has faded with time (plates 12, 13). Contemporary observers admired a "prismatic lustre" produced by the optical fusion of colors embedded in the brick surfaces. In fact, they described such an effect impressionistically: "when seen from a distance, all the colors blend into a general impression of soft red and green, while at close range they maintain their individuality."[24] This description gives further evidence that Sullivan proceeded like an Impressionist painter: he enhanced dominantly reddish brick hues with a subordinate palette of contrasting and analogous colors and tones. He devised this chromatic composition by using secondary facing materials and ornamentation: mottled green, buff-yellow, or burnt-orange terra cotta reliefs; predominantly blue or green mosaic panels; dark green marble; and bronze or gold leaf.

Under the best conditions of patronage, Sullivan increased the range of polychromatic materials for the bank interiors. He produced dominant color harmonies of golden browns and yellow- and blue-greens to suggest conditions of autumn or spring on an open prairie field or under the canopy of a forest interior. The main auditorium of the Auditorium Building (1886–89) and the Trading Room of the Stock Exchange Building (1894) exemplify Sullivan's earlier efforts to achieve these naturalistic decorative programs.[25] For the National Farmers' Bank interior he exceeded these previous schemes (figures 8–10; plates 2–4).

When designing the interior of the National Farmers' Bank, Sullivan emphasized that he wanted to make "the out of doors—indoors." He discussed how he intended to translate his personal synaesthetic experience and renderings of the landscape into "a color symphony with the many shades of the strings and the woodwinds and the brass."[26] That is, Sullivan wanted to represent natural conditions with color harmonies that simultaneously evoked rhythmic musical harmonies.[27] Here, and in the ensuing banks, Sullivan combined the earth tones of speckled glazed brick and stained oak woodwork with the verdant hues of dark green marble and mosaic tiles. Sullivan further orchestrated the colors of nature with light emitted from a variety of sources: chromatic light from brilliant patterns of opalescent and stained glass windows; tinted natural light from skylights; golden artificial light from incandescent light bulbs; and reflected light from bronze, gilded, or glazed relief surfaces. Viewed together in any one bank interior, these chromatic combinations permeate spaces with shifting rhythms of lights and shadows and of warm and cool tones.

In the National Farmers' Bank Sullivan translated his organic mode of ornament into two-dimensional stencil patterns and gilded and glazed relief enframements. Rendered in complementary and analogous color combinations of orange, yellow, green, and blue, the polychromatic frescoes produce a dominantly green ambience to which all other polychromatic materials are subordinated. Similar to the effects of optical blending produced by the tinted brick exteriors, the colors of the fresco patterns interact to dissolve and make diaphonous the surfaces they adorn. Sullivan also incorporated actual natural processes into his color scheme. At different times of the day or the year, the prevailing color tones shift from yellowish burnt orange-green to blue-green. These interior changes are caused by the transient effects of outdoor light. Here, in his most complete bank interior, Sullivan most effectively harmonized nature and art.[28]

"Form Follows Function" and the Function of the "Democratic Plan"

Sullivan developed for the banks what he called the "democratic plan." While the formal elements of such a plan belong to nineteenth-century academic conventions, its theory and design are based on Sullivan's credo "form follows function" and the twofold meanings he assigned those terms. As I will show, Sullivan extended this natural law from the skyscrapers to the banks in order to clarify and thereby democratize the purposeful arrangement of the parts to the whole.[29]

Sullivan began his design process with nineteenth-century academic methods of composition.[30] These methods for rationalist planning provided the means for arranging a variety of functional spaces in a hierarchical order along parallel and symmetrical cross-axes. Sullivan had conceived such simple axial layouts for the mercantile and office spaces of his skyscraper designs, schemes he first refined in the Wainwright Building. In each of the rural town banks Sullivan placed the main banking area on the major axis and surrounded or aligned it with subordinate working and meeting spaces: tellers' cages, officers' and secretarial quarters, men's and women's restrooms, and community meeting rooms (figures 12, 14, 31, 41, 49).[31] Because each of these spaces is within clear view or easy access, the spectator/user gains an immediate awareness of the practical efficiency of the plan (figures 8–10, 32, 48a, 49, 60, 64). Here, too, Sullivan drew on his earlier experiences as a designer of multi-use commercial buildings. We can return to the Auditorium Building, the Wainwright Building, and the Guaranty Building to see how he had designed open plans for banks and other communal spaces enclosed on the first two stories of the base of his three-part skyscraper scheme.

Sometimes Sullivan's clients determined an arrangement of functional spaces that best suited their own practical concerns. Such conditions prevailed in the Owatonna Bank commission. But in his second bank, the Peoples Savings Bank in Cedar Rapids, Iowa (1909–10), Sullivan realized more fully the implications of the democratic plan.[32] In his description of this bank, he joined his organic metaphor for "form follows function" with a mechanistic one to establish his rationalist methods for rendering the bank's functional appearance:

The exterior is . . . the logical outcome of the plan, the building designed from within, outward, the prime governing considerations being utilitarian—that is, an effort was made to secure a banking layout especially adapted to its class of business, and which would be, as nearly as possible, an automatically working machine.[33]

As can still be seen on the exterior, Sullivan clearly articulated the interior layout with simple, geometric masses incised with deep-set windows and entrance (figures 14–18). Sullivan did not intend this visual representation of the organic-mechanistic metaphor to be an end in itself. Rather, he assigned it a social, as opposed to a strictly architectural, function to advance the progress of democracy. He designated this function in his account of the interior layout:

The highpoint of interest is the interior. It was designed, with all its adjuncts, strictly as a banking room. Its plan may be called "democratic", in that the prospect is open and the offices are in plain view and easily apprehended. This may be called the modern "human" element of the plan, as it tends to promote a feeling of ease, confidence, and friendship between officers, employees, and customers.[34]

In the bank at Cedar Rapids, Sullivan reinforced the social function of the democratic plan by replacing the foliate grillwork, used in the Owatonna bank, with continuous vertical bronze grilles (figures 21, 22). Sullivan designed these grilles to screen, but not obscure, the tellers' work spaces and the vaults from the public banking area. For the officers' and secretaries' quarters opposite the tellers' area, he left the space above the counters completely open. Sullivan accentuated this open spatial arrangement with backlighting from a horizontal range of windows behind the tellers' area. With this arrangement of space and light, Sullivan made almost every banking activity immediately visible. In the bank interiors that followed, he further minimized visual obstacles between the workers' and patrons' spaces by replacing grilles with polished glass partitions joined by small bronze clamps (figures 44, 48a).

Because the interior of the Peoples Savings Bank has been drastically altered, Montgomery Schuyler's observations of the original layout are especially useful for appreciating Sullivan's mastery of the open plan. Schuyler identified the open plan as a modern innovation in bank design. He also recognized that Sullivan went beyond the example of his contemporaries by exploiting its visual accessibility. Schuyler took delight in viewing the unconventional expanse of the open plan:

Whoever enters the Cedar Rapids bank can see through it from end to end and from side to side. Even the vault is thrown open during business hours and becomes an impressive element in the architectural ensemble.[35]

And when Schuyler claimed that with this bold gesture Sullivan had effectively lifted the "veil" between banker and clients, he corroborated the democratic social meanings Sullivan ascribed to the practical and psychological elements of the open plan.

Schuyler's remarks indicate that Sullivan succeeded in communicating to his contemporaries that the open democratic plan was "a complete inversion of the traditional notion of what a bank should be." In his description of the Cedar Rapids bank, Sullivan explained how to read such an "inversion": first, he rid the bank of its traditional classical temple form; second, he eliminated compartmentalized banking facilities. These traditional arrangements, Sullivan argued, shrouded financial transactions in darkness, imposing on banking the mystery of pagan rituals.[36]

Sullivan may have demystified the "pagan" ritual of banking, but in his democratic layouts he made this commercial enterprise continuous with a spiritual experience in nature. In the notations on his plans and in the distribution of light and space, Sullivan suggested that he conceived the banks as arenas for secularized liturgical events.

Neither Sullivan's contemporaries nor recent historians have overlooked his overt references to ecclesiastical architecture in his blueprints.[37] Terms such as "clerestory" and "side aisle" recall the spatial distributions of a church plan. But Sullivan devised more explicit liturgical references for the spectator/user's actual encounter with these spaces. He set the stage for a ceremonial procession into and through the banks by arranging alternating sequences of low, dark areas with high, brightly lit spaces. Upon entering each of the banks, the spectator/user passes from daylight into a low, dark vestibule. Leaving this transitional space, the individual encounters the opposite effect in the main banking area. The banking hall, where "clerestory" or "rose" windows and skylights chromatically illuminate two-story elevations, immediately recalls the ambience of a church nave (plates 4, 7, 13). Sullivan strengthened this allusion by surrounding the square or elongated banking hall with "side aisles" serving subordinate work and office spaces (figures 8–10, 22–24, 31, 32, 41, 49, 50, 60).

Finally, while Sullivan fostered his patrons' pride in their monumental, mechanized vaults, he converted their materialistic conceit into reverential awe. Whenever possible, Sullivan aligned the vault with the entrance

Sullivan's Shift from Transcendental Idealism to Pragmatist Realism

at the opposite end of the main axis. He developed this layout most extensively in the Peoples Savings and Loan Association (1917–18; figures 48a, 48b), where the vault door is viewed through an uninterrupted partition of polished plate glass. When the door is open, the vault's deep cavernous opening, gleaming metal surfaces, and radiating lock patterns inevitably invoke associations with sacramental altars.

Thus far I have shown that Sullivan selected various artistic conventions to communicate his participation in a transcendentalist philosophical discourse: he used symbolic forms and artistic techniques to make the real ideal. I now want to describe how certain formal changes in the banks coincide with changes in Sullivan's extra-architectural values and concepts; these formal changes correlate with Sullivan's verbal statements denoting his intellectual shift from transcendentalist idealism to pragmatist realism.

Viewed in the context of Sullivan's complete works, the bank designs mark the culmination of a shift in his procedures for combining ornament with tectonic features. For the Guaranty Building elevations (1894–95), Sullivan had achieved a subtle blending of red terra cotta ornamental reliefs and simple rectangular massing enframing attenuated structural (and nonstructural) piers. With the Gage Building facade (1898) and then the Schlesinger-Mayer Store (1898, 1902–3), Sullivan began to disengage the subjective-organic and the objective-geometric components of his designs.[38] He contrasted large-scale organic ornament with equally scaled geometric masses and primary architectural forms.

This formal shift coincides with Sullivan's involvement with a new school of thought, that of "Chicago School" pragmatism. Pragmatist teachings were transmitted from the University of Chicago beginning in 1894, two years after the institution officially opened its doors. During its so-called "golden" decade of 1894–1904, "Chicago School" pragmatism was hailed as an indigenous, progressive, and democratic interdisciplinary discourse.[39] Pragmatism not only confirmed Sullivan's earlier transcendentalist beliefs,[40] it also helped him to reshape his architectural means of representation to communicate his own democratic ideals and behavior. The basic principles of the pragmatist system suggest that Sullivan deliberately juxtaposed reductivist mass with boldly rendered ornament. These principles provided him with a method for differentiating functionalist open plans from naturalistic decorative programs and then assigning to both schemes democratic social meanings.

Chicago School pragmatism began as an attack on abstract conceptual constructs that isolated philosophy and ethics from the concrete realities of human life.[41] To close this gap, the pragmatists devised a dynamic, open-ended continuum between thought and action and between theory and practice. Under John Dewey's leadership, administered from the university's department of education, professors from almost every academic field exhibited pragmatist thought in their pedagogical actions. As teachers at the university's experimental elementary school, as public lecturers, and as civic leaders and officials, these academicians disseminated pragmatist ideology and models for social behavior into the nonacademic community. They claimed that this kind of beneficent social activity would guarantee the progressive, albeit organic, evolution of democracy.

To substantiate their theory-practice continuum, the pragmatists joined a biological model of organic functionalism to the methods of scientific experimentation. They argued that the actively thinking being, like any other organism, is shaped by and shapes the environments he or she encounters in problem-solving situations. The pragmatists promoted individual growth that occurs through direct interaction with nature and with society, experiences that lead to critical self-reflection, and a continuous testing of internal against external realities. They taught that individual organic growth results in organic social change. When the pragmatists applied the biological model and experimental methods to

the progress of democracy, it became morally imperative that the individual clearly and openly address and attempt to solve the problems of human existence and social bonding.

While the biological-functionalist model reinforced Sullivan's organic-rationalist theories of design, the socialized scientific model identified an agenda for enacting his philosophical values. Thus, Sullivan's clarification of the practical/objective and the spiritual/subjective components of his bank designs must be considered a mode of social activity directed toward the attainment of a transcendental democracy. Furthermore, the new formal clarity that appears in the banks coincides with similar stylistic and thematic shifts in his theoretical writings. This rhetorical shift, in fact, dates from 1894 and constitutes a move away from his earlier suggestive, lyrical prose style, a style derived from Whitman's poetry and prose, toward greater didactic clarity and directness.[42] Sullivan's fully developed pragmatist attitudes finally emerged in the essay "What is Architecture: A Study in the American People of Today." Written in 1906 and published in *The Craftsman,* this article is especially noteworthy in relation to the history of the banks. Carl Bennett, Sullivan's first rural bank client, commissioned Sullivan to design a new building for his financial institution after he read this article.[43]

In "What is Architecture" Sullivan proposed a new, democratic system of architectural criticism grounded in what he called "natural thinking" and its pragmatist corollary, the organic reciprocity between thought and action. He instructed the reader of his text on how to become a reader of his buildings. The process begins with a reeducation in nature, during which the novice abandons all false ideas about what constitutes "good taste" in architecture.

Sullivan used the concept of natural thinking to connect the transcendentalist real-ideal continuum with the pragmatist thought-action continuum. First, he made natural thinking a means for reading his symbolic language of architecture. Sullivan explained that before the reader becomes a critic, he must learn to read architecture as the poet reads natural appearances; that is, as the outward symbols of the spiritual ideal. Following this primary lesson in nature, Sullivan made natural thinking the critical faculty for discerning good from bad architecture, or "democratic" from "feudal" architecture.[44] He instructed his reader to read architecture critically, using a method for testing internal with external realities based on the premise "as Man thinks, so he acts" and its corollary "each building stands as a social act." At the end of this learning process the newly trained reader-critic would be able to test the moral integrity of the architect by the readability and simplicity of his designs.

The purpose of this exegesis on popular criticism was to reconsider how reductivist architectural imagery becomes the sign of the architect's beneficent social acts. Sullivan wrote that the primordial elements of architecture—the "pier, lintel, and arch"—are analogous to the poet's word-symbols.[45] He thereby identified these elements as the timeless symbols with which all true architects have recorded the most profound human insights of nature's processes.

Sullivan further revealed his pragmatist strategy when he claimed that by way of natural thinking the reader-critic will learn to participate in "the art of reading . . . as a science, an art of interpretation," and thereby "close the illogical gap between the theoretical and practical."[46] Sullivan denounced academic instruction for widening such a gap. He argued that by teaching the outward forms of revival styles that had no relation to the realities of American life, academics severed architecture from its vital origins. To close this gap between architecture and life, Sullivan concluded his essay with a test that examines both the makers and users of architecture against a Whitmanesque "democratic vista." He claimed any individual could participate in the progress of transcendental democracy: since natural thinking is a democratic critical system, it is accessible to everyone. Indeed, Sullivan prophesied that "the American people will make Democracy a religion" when maker and user reject styles of taste and abstract learning and instead create and demand an architecture shaped by human and natural conditions.[47]

In his own artistic procedures and problem-solving techniques for his bank designs, Sullivan attempted to present two correlated models for democratic social action. As an image-maker for democracy, he clarified the parts of his designs to denote the integrity of his own social actions. That is, in the process of inverting traditional bank layouts, Sullivan demonstrated his belief in "the social fact . . . that banking is a function of society and not a secluded mystery apart from the people."[48] As a symbol-maker for democracy, he arranged each banking space to provoke the spectator/user's reflection upon his or her social and organic bonds. Sullivan assumed that when self-reflection is joined with aesthetic contemplation, the individual would apprehend how practical needs and utilitarian functions are one with nature's processes and democracy's progress.

Making the Real Ideal: Arts and Crafts Design, Lighting, and Technology

As I have just argued, Sullivan used practical, functional solutions as points of departure for communicating metaphysical values and ideal social behavior. The banks, even more than the skyscrapers, exemplify his procedures for creating, in his own words, "an indigenous American style by deifying the commonplace."[49] But to realize this comprehensive program, he relied on a team of technical and artistic collaborators who worked in a wide range of media. Such a collaboration has led present-day scholars to question the authorship of parts of his designs and, in turn, to attribute these parts to Sullivan's assistants.[50]

For reconstructing Sullivan's working procedures the validity of such attributions cannot be denied. Sullivan's chief draftsmen were always responsible for transcribing his preliminary sketches into working and presentation drawings.[51] George Grant Elmslie, chief draftsman between 1893 and 1909, assisted Sullivan in designing the facade and the relief motifs for the bank in Owatonna (figure 6; plates 2, 3).[52] Likewise, Parker N. Berry, who succeeded Elmslie and remained with Sullivan until 1917, completed Sullivan's designs for the Land and Loan Office in Algona, Iowa (1913–14; figures 25, 26) and the Purdue State Bank in West Lafayette, Indiana (1914; figure 29).[53] Louis J. Millet and Kristian Schneider assisted Sullivan throughout his career in the realization of his naturalistic decorative schemes. Millet, an eminent architectural decorator and teacher at The Art Institute of Chicago,[54] translated Sullivan's personal mode of organic ornament into frescoes, mosaics, and leaded stained glass. Schneider, a freelance clay modeler for the American Terra Cotta Company, a firm that manufactured Sullivan's reliefs for most of the banks, shaped Sullivan's two-dimensional drawings for ornament into three-dimensional models for casting in plaster, metal, and terra cotta.[55]

Scholars who attribute parts of Sullivan's designs to his assistants often deprive Sullivan of what he and his contemporaries considered the most important part of realizing a work of art. Sullivan's involvement with transcendentalist philosophy aligned him with a nineteenth-century romantic tradition that regarded the artist's emotional, intuitive conception of the work of art as the most original, authentic, and seminal phase of the creative process. This instinctive phase was followed by the artist's rational selection of the artistic means and materials of representation. Adherents to this precept would claim that in the final work of art, the artist joined intuition and reason to communicate his original source of inspiration to the spectator.[56]

Statements by Sullivan's contemporaries provide evidence for understanding his artistic methods in the context of this tradition. While his reviewers frequently cited the specific contributions of his collaborators, at the time no one, not even the collaborators, questioned Sullivan's primary authorship.[57] Consequently, Sullivan deserves full credit for composing what was described and experienced by his contemporaries as a total work of art. In his own time, Sullivan's artistic individuality and originality were equated with just such a holistic integration of utilitarian and decorative features.

Questions concerning who designed and executed particular fragments of the bank designs simply become less important when it is understood how Sullivan conceived, selected, and rendered each part in relation to the whole. For example, Sullivan's incorporation of interior furnishings into the overall design of the banks is one of his most important artistic choices. This choice indicates his participation in the Chicago Arts and Crafts movement. Late-nineteenth-century Arts and

Crafts values and design principles complemented Sullivan's pragmatist tasks, helping him to integrate more completely the images of transcendentalist idealism with technological and utilitarian realism.

At the turn of the twentieth-century, progressive American architects and designers appropriated English Arts and Crafts theories and art forms for their own aesthetic ends.[58] First defined by William Morris in the 1860s, Arts and Crafts ideals were subsequently disseminated in the United States by his "Craftsman" followers, especially through the artistic and literary activities of Gustav Stickley.[59] Within these English and American traditions, artists and architects collaborated with local craftsmen to create architectural environments as complete works of art and to break the boundaries between the utilitarian, applied, and fine arts.

Sullivan became directly involved with American Arts and Crafts or Craftsman movement in 1905, if not before.[60] At that time, Stickley, as editor of *The Craftsman,* reprinted Sullivan's 1896 essay "The Tall Office Building Artistically Considered" as "Form and Function Artistically Considered." In the next year Stickley published "What is Architecture: A Study of the American People Today." Sullivan reciprocated Stickley's support and affirmed their shared Arts and Crafts values by introducing Craftsman style furnishings in his first bank interior.

For the National Farmers' Bank in Owatonna, and for the succeeding banks, Sullivan designed the interiors either entirely or partially in the Craftsman style.[61] Built-in and freestanding desks, chairs, settles, storage cabinets, display cases, and bookshelves, frequently detailed with Sullivan's organic ornament, exhibit typical Arts and Crafts features (figures 5, 8–11, 22–24, 33–36, 38, 44, 48a, 50, 51, 60, 65). These furnishings are characterized by an immediately visible clarity of purpose, construction,

and materials. Sullivan employed the natural materials and simple rectilinear outlines of the Craftsman style to harmonize utilitarian objects with the dimensions and contours of the structural elements and elevations of the bank interiors. In the same way, he harmonized the hues of the furniture with the hues of the woodwork and wood veneers. Whenever possible Sullivan stained quarter-sawn white oak with what was called a "Craftsman style finish," a treatment that gave the wood a green or grayish-green hue (figures 13, 65).[62] With these techniques, Sullivan fully coordinated the natural wood textures and tones to the overall naturalistic ambience of the bank interiors (plate 15).

Unlike his American followers, William Morris reluctantly and cautiously gave the machine a limited place in the execution of his designs. Like his American colleagues, Sullivan more fully embraced technology as a means for creating a total work of art. But Sullivan closely followed Morris's Arts and Crafts values for social reform: he conceived his furnishings to be an integral part of an organic, life-enhancing environment. And he agreed with Morris that such a setting would shape the intellectual and physical conditions for social progress. Indeed, Sullivan included Craftsman designs in his architectural schemes to indicate yet another aspect of his pragmatist activities and his related efforts to create an American style. In Morris's program Sullivan would have found further justification for his attempts to create a democratic art form. Like Sullivan, Morris and his followers argued that the true principles of design resided in nature rather than in the mechanical reproduction of historical styles.[63] Since the straightforward simplicity of Craftsman designs are grounded in these naturalistic theories, they provided Sullivan with visual and conceptual analogues of his democratic plan.

Sullivan selected and incorporated more overt utilitarian elements—steel-frame construction, double-glazed windows, lighting, and heating, air-conditioning, and ventilating systems—into his organic plans and artistic compositions. His ability to combine utility and art is due, in part, to his participation in the Arts and Crafts movement during the later part of his career. But Sullivan succeeded in enhancing decorative with structural forms and transcendentalist symbol-making with practical demands in the banks because he had already done so in the skyscrapers. In fact, in 1916, the year that he began the Sidney, Ohio, bank project, Sullivan had an occasion to write a history of the Chicago School architects' development of commercial buildings.

Originally delivered as an address and then published as an article, Sullivan's "Development of Construction"[64] provides a basis for determining which utilitarian and decorative techniques Sullivan extended from the urban building type to the small town rural bank. Improved ventilating, cooling, and heating systems, fireproof construction, large panes of plate glass, and hardwood finish carried throughout the buildings were among those novel techniques that he credited to his earlier collaboration with Dankmar Adler. He also identified Adler's contributions to the development of structural foundations and steel-frame construction for skyscrapers and of the multi-use commercial buildings. Yet Sullivan took sole credit for "developing a little technical knowledge [him]self," what he (modestly) described as "the first decorative use of the electric lamp." He further explained, "It was a little innovation of my own, that of placing the lamps in a decoration instead of clustering them in[side] fixtures."[65] This latter development is especially important in considering how Sullivan assimilated the more overtly utilitarian features into an overall naturalistic scheme. But Sullivan's statements also remind us that when he transferred those late nineteenth-century utilitarian forms to the rural setting during the first decades of the twentieth century, local observers had never seen them before; they were therefore impressed by the novelty and economy of such standard practical conveniences.[66]

Sullivan primarily employed brick, cast-iron, and concrete construction for the smaller scale of the banks. Occasionally, however, he did use components and principles of the skeletal steel-frame construction he had mastered in the skyscraper. As in the skyscrapers, he used this modern building technique to accommodate economic and practical needs, especially for reducing the density and closure of non-load-bearing walls and for open, flexible plans. But he also used the steel frame in the skyscraper to exaggerate verticality as a sign of human spiritual aspirations.[67] In a similar way, Sullivan took advantage of steel construction in the banks to augment his efforts to communicate his social and aesthetic ideals. When he adapted to the banks the steel post-and-beam system, which allowed him to span wide spaces with minimal support, Sullivan could more fully develop both open spaces and extensive fenestration, features that are intrinsic to the democratic plan and his naturalist aesthetics (figures 48a, 49, 61, 62).[68]

Sullivan likewise combined the decorative functions and naturalistic associations of diffused chromatic lights with a highly practical treatment of illumination. He arranged skylights and window-walls to admit an abundance of natural light into the public banking and subordinate service spaces (figures 11, 17, 22). This upper-level or second-story illumination flooded the main-story spaces, which Sullivan often designed without ceilings. Instead, he rendered a skeletal post-and-beam system in wood and brick to mark off the varied spaces on the ground floor without interrupting the uniform radiance emitted from above (figures 9, 32, 34, 36, 48a, 50, 51, 60, 64). He also designed artificial lighting to enrich chromatic harmonies and to facilitate eyesight in more specialized work areas. Following his earlier innovations in decorative lighting, Sullivan surrounded ornamental electroliers and skylights with tiny incandescent bulbs, adding a subtle scintillation to gilded and glazed relief surfaces (figures 9, 10, 22, 23, 32; plates 2, 3, 6). He also embedded frosted glass fixtures in ceilings and in reflecting bronze troughs within architraves over tellers' cages and officers' quarters to provide stronger direct lighting for practical use. In addition, he attached unadorned globe bulbs to walls and placed leaded, opalescent glass lamps on desks as direct lighting for more detailed work by both patrons and employees (figures 13, 24, 38, 44, 45). These and the other more utilitarian lights mix with diffused daylight to spread a softly modulated luminance throughout the banks' interiors.

Sullivan's use of polished plate glass was one of the most innovative features in the bank designs. In the Guaranty Building he had exploited this mechanically refined material for artistic and practical purposes.[69] There he surrounded the entire ground story of the street elevations with polished plate glass, exposing decorated freestanding structural piers. On the interior, daylight flooded a single-room banking space that occupied the building's northeast corner. The interior glazed partitions of this room opened onto the central vestibule, exposing an autumnal decorative scheme of marble, mosaics, and bronze electroplated relief elevator grilles. (Leaded stained glass skylights enhanced this golden ambience in the rear lobby.) For the interior of the rural town banks Sullivan resumed his innovative use of large glass panes. He installed continuous glass partitions between public and business spaces to complete the democratization of the open plan (figures 44, 48a, 64; plate 15). If for security's sake Sullivan had to impose an actual separation between client and teller or vault, he left intact a full view of both the mechanical and human aspects of banking rites.

Sullivan also used plate glass windows for combined practical and aesthetic ends. He inserted panels of polished plate glass into the exterior walls to protect the leaded glass windows. At the same time, he modulated the chromatic intensity of stained glass against the dominant red tones of the brick elevations. Sullivan also employed this double-glazing technique to seal an intervening air space, providing an insulation system for year-round temperature control throughout the bank interiors (figure 11; plates 11, 13, 15).[70]

Sullivan's critics and clients consistently praised him for bringing innovative mechanical equipment into his designs to solve practical requirements of the building program. His schemes for heating, cooling, and ventilating systems were frequently cited by local observers as the most outstanding of these technological accomplishments. For many of the banks, Sullivan transferred from his skyscraper designs a sophisticated air-conditioning system that operated on a combination of forced, recycled air and rainwater. Such a system proved to be an economic and efficient component of the self-contained temperature control system and, more recently, to be easily convertible to modern air-conditioning technology (figures 14, 41, 49).[71]

A variety of practical features in each bank also helps to demonstrate how Sullivan continued to integrate utility with art in the minor details. In

Sullivan as Image-Maker for Democracy: Rural Clients and Rural Main Street

public banking spaces he housed ventilation air ducts within the piers that mark the major and minor axes of the plan (figures 48a, 49). He also enclosed radiators within the built-in furniture to alleviate potentially obtrusive technological display (figure 44). In the Peoples Savings and Loan Association at Sidney, he concealed radiators inside slab marble benches aligned with the plan's central axis (figure 48a). Elsewhere in this bank he exhibited an alternative for making the real ideal. He revealed the sculptural elegance of technological form by enframing radiators within rectangular niches precisely cut into the brick wall.

How well did Sullivan communicate his philosophical and social ideals to the layperson? Professional criticism and discussions of the banks in local newspapers and bank brochures suggest that Sullivan's rural clients sanctioned what they regarded as the democratic meanings of his architectural forms. Thomas Tallmadge believed Sullivan met his clients' expectations and values: he wrote that while Montgomery Schuyler claimed each bank was an "architectural event" for the professional architect, each bank more importantly marked "an event in the life of the American citizen."[72] Sullivan's success as an image-maker for democracy can be measured, in part, by inquiring into the significance of this "event." This inquiry entails a review of the conditions that made it possible for a rural population to reclaim Sullivan after he had been rejected by his urban clients.

During the heyday of Sullivan's career as a designer of skyscrapers, urban speculators endorsed his innovative designs because progressive architectural imagery matched their own innovative business practices. But following the 1893 Chicago World's Fair, popular tastes shifted in favor of the classical revival styles that adorned the "White City," the monumental centerpiece of the fairgrounds. Midwestern urban speculators began to commission classical revival style designs for their steel-framed skyscrapers. This shift from a preference for progressive to revival styles was more than a matter of taste. It was also governed by the cultural associations that each style signified. Academic classicism represented timeless artistic values of Western civilization and, in turn, an ancient tradition of logic extended into modern financial planning. Sullivan's original style, his rejection of the temple form, and his technological expertise connoted progressive, democratic ideals and business practices born in the "new world." It was this latter stylistic association that made possible Sullivan's commissions for midwestern rural banks.

At the turn of the century, locally financed banking institutions grew rapidly in response to agricultural, commercial, and industrial expansion in the rural midwest. Savings and loan associations emerged as a new enterprise in American banking. We thus can assume that the progressive rural bankers who founded these institutions celebrated their independence from their urban counterparts by appropriating Sullivan's innovative architectural and technological forms. If Sullivan's strongest supporters occasionally had to counter their more conservative colleagues' preferences for classical temple forms, his defenders prevailed.[73] The most outspoken among his clients, they were confident that Sullivan's logical plans, modern construction, and artistic decoration offered opportunities for a wise economic investment. In most cases they were right to argue that a bank by Sullivan would attract new customers and foster financial growth.

Sullivan made himself eminently affordable for even the most limited building budgets. Although Sullivan's national and international fame made him an instant celebrity in rural areas, he was not impervious to self-advertisement. On the correspondence side of a photographic postcard of the Merchants National Bank in Grinnell, Iowa (figure 5), Sullivan inscribed for his clients in Sidney, Ohio, what he likely regarded as the building's vital statistics:

Bank Building for the Merchants' Nat'l Bank
Grinnell, Iowa
Size: 42′ × 75′ Cost $60,000
Louis H. Sullivan Archt
Chicago.

Sullivan's rural clients expressed their democratic attitudes in other ways that are consistent with the era's progressive social values. In assuming the role of civic leader, these bankers considered the construction of Sullivan's "jewel boxes" an event that fulfilled their self-assigned duty to modernize and embellish their civic townscapes and to ameliorate public conveniences. It was by way of such social gestures that we can speculate about Sullivan's rural clients' participation in the City Beautiful movement.[74] At the turn of the century, the City Beautiful movement took shape as a loose coalition of architects, city officials, city planners, and businessmen who sought to modernize and impose order on towns and cities that had grown haphazardly under the impact of rapid industrial and commercial expansion. More often than not, comprehensive projects for civic improvement remained on the drawing board. But piecemeal projects for commercial, religious, and public buildings were built. Sullivan's banks are among these smaller accomplishments of City Beautiful schemes.

As the anonymous reviewer I cited at the beginning of this survey observed, Sullivan composed each bank as a complete, self-referential work of art and he harmonized each work within the townscape. In this latter effort Sullivan followed the best traditions of civic design. He conformed to the constraints imposed by the building site and by his clients. Each of Sullivan's banks is located at major Main Street intersections,[75] a site rural bankers typically chose to designate the bank's preeminence in town life as a locus of commercial, civic, and social amenities.

Sullivan's problem of civic design thus was twofold: he had to integrate and then monumentalize his banks within the fabric of rural Main Streets. Local histories record that Sullivan sketched elevations directly

5
Merchants National Bank, vintage post-card, signed by Louis H. Sullivan, ca. 1916. Courtesy of Ferdinand E. Freytag, FAIA.

at the proposed building site. During this process he created a dialogue between the banks and their given architectural settings. As the Grinnell postcard makes clear, he incorporated into his elevations the delineations, dimensions, rhythms, textures, materials, and colors of the existing buildings (figures 7, 46). By varying the combination of these elements for each bank, Sullivan addressed both adjacent commercial building fronts and the nineteenth-century revival styles of civic monuments located on sites opposite the banks.

Each bank nonetheless remains a monument in its own right. Sullivan did not achieve monumentality by enlarging the scale of the banks in relation to the built environment. Rather, he achieved this grandeur by emphasizing the geometric simplicity of rectangular masses that seem to rise from the grid of the street. As a result, each bank gives an ordered closure to the irregular accretion of buildings that line the commercial blocks.

Notes

1.

"Recent Bank Buildings of the United States," *Architectural Record* 25 (January 1909): 8.

2.

A. N. Rebori, "The Architecture of Democracy: Three Recent Examples of the Work of Louis Sullivan," *Architectural Record* 39 (May 1916): 436–65.

3.

Ibid., 437–38.

4.

Ibid., 438.

5.

Ibid.

6.

Only a few among Sullivan's colleagues understood the metaphysical underpinnings of his theory and design. See, for example, Claude Bragdon, "An American Architect: Being an Appreciation of Louis H. Sullivan," *House and Garden* 7 (January 1905): 47–55; Louis J. Millet, "The National Farmers' Bank of Owatonna, Minn.," *Architectural Record* 24 (October 1908): 248–55; Frank Lloyd Wright, review of Morrison's *Louis Sullivan* in *The Saturday Review of Literature*, 14 December 1935, rpt. *Journal of the Society of Architectural Historians* 20 (October 1961): 140–41; and George Elmslie's response to Wright's review in a 12 June 1936 letter, reprinted in the *JSAH* with Wright's critique. Years later Wright wrote extensively on Sullivan's metaphysical beliefs; see *Genius and the Mobocracy* (1949; rpt. New York: Horizon, 1971).

7.

In his autobiography Sullivan complained that only a few of his peers responded sympathetically to his first metaphysical tract, "Inspiration" (1886), when he read it at the convention of the Western Association of Architects in 1886. See Sullivan's *Autobiography of an Idea* (1924; rpt. New York: Dover, 1956), p. 302.

8.

Ralph Waldo Emerson, "The Poet" (1844) in *Essays: Second Series*, Vol. 3 of *Complete Works* (Boston and New York: Houghton Mifflin & Co., 1903), p. 13.

Sullivan as a transcendentalist thinker is the subject of Sherman Paul's monograph, *Louis Sullivan: An Architect in American Thought* (Englewood Cliffs: Prentice-Hall, 1962). Paul was one of the first scholars to seriously examine Sullivan's place within a nineteenth-century American intellectual tradition. For an explanation of how Sullivan translated transcendentalist philosophical concepts and literary forms into a means of architectural representation see my article, "Naturalized Technology: Louis Sullivan's Whitmanesque Skyscrapers," *Centennial Review* 30 (Fall 1986), 480–95.

9.

See Sullivan, "Ornament in Architecture" (1892); "Emotional Architecture as Compared with Intellectual" (1894); "The Tall Office Building Artistically Considered" (1896); "The Elements of Architecture: Objective and Subjective (1) Pier and Lintel" and "(2) The Arch" from *Kindergarten Chats* (1901; 1918) in *Kindergarten Chats (1918) and Other Writings*, ed. Isabella Athey (New York: Wittenborn, 1947) and *A System of Architectural Ornament According with a Philosophy of Man's Powers* (1924; New York: The Eakins Press, 1967).

Sullivan first realized this opposition and synthesis of geometric and botanical motifs in designs for ornament dating from 1885. However, it was not until the Wainwright Building (1890) that he extended this means of representation to his complete architectural compositions. For a discussion of Sullivan's stylistic development of ornament, see Paul E. Sprague, *The Drawings of Louis Henry Sullivan: A Catalogue of the Frank Lloyd Wright Collection at the Avery Architectural Library* (Princeton: Princeton University Press, 1979), pp. 4–8 and esp. cat. no. 24.

10.

Sullivan, "Emotional Architecture as Compared with Intellectual," 194.

11.

Sullivan, "The Tall Office Building Artistically Considered," 206. Cf. n. 7 above; Wright criticized Morrison for misrepresenting Sullivan "as the forerunner of a functionalism for which neither then—nor now, would he have ever had more than a curse." Wright further implied that Adler adhered to the mechanistic-functionalist meaning of "form follows function." Such a meaning is distinct from Sullivan's and more directly related to Horatio Greenough's earlier theories of functionalism. For an attempt to distinguish between the "vitalistic" and "mechanistic" meanings of functionalism, see Donald Drew Egbert, "The Idea of Organic Expression and American Architecture," *Evolutionary Thought in America*, ed. Stow Persons (New Haven: Yale University Press, 1950); and Paul E. Sprague, "The Architectural Ornament of Louis Sullivan and his Chief Draftsmen," Ph.D. Dissertation, Princeton University, 1969, ch. I.

12.

Sullivan, "Tall Office Building," 207–8.

13.

Sullivan, *Kindergarten Chats* (1918), p. 46.

14.

According to William Presto, Sullivan's assistant draftsman for the Farmers and Merchants Union Bank in Columbus, Wisconsin, Sullivan was also working on a bank for Manistique, Michigan, during this time. See Bernard C. Greengard, "Sullivan/Presto/The Kraus Music Store," *The Prairie School Review* 6 (Third Quarter 1969): 6, n. 6. More recently, it has been determined that this was a remodeling project which was never realized. In a letter to Frank Lloyd Wright dated 4 April 1920, Sullivan wrote, "Have been at work on a hurry up bank remodeling job at Manistique, Mich.—a good plan, but a potboiler otherwise" (cited from *Frank Lloyd Wright: Letters to Architects*, ed. Bruce Brooks Pfeiffer [Fresno: The Press at California State University, Fresno, 1984], p. 17). For an extant drawing for this project, see Sprague, *The Drawings of Louis Sullivan*, figure 59 ("Horizontal section through main supply duct near ceiling," 12 February 1920).

15.

Thomas Tallmadge, "The Farmers' and Merchants' Bank of Columbus, Wisconsin," *The Western Architect* 29 (July 1920): 63.

16.

Ibid.

17.

See Sullivan, "Suggestions in Artistic Brickwork" (1910); rpt. *The Prairie School Review* 4 (Second Quarter): 24–26.

18.
In "Suggestions in Artistic Brickwork" Sullivan used the term "tint" in a painterly way, implying the overall effects as an end result, rather than the actual means of using highly saturated individual bricks. As Crombie Taylor explains (personal conversation with author, December 1983), Sullivan took advantage of the natural gain of intense coloration during the firing process. That is, depending on the distance of the bricks from the heat source and the walls of the kiln, the oxides will burn at varied speeds, producing a wide range of hues. Tallmadge labeled the medium "tapestry brick," a phrase that has persisted in descriptions of the banks; see Tallmadge, *The Story of Architecture in America* (New York: W. W. Norton and Co., 1927), p. 225. Sullivan's first known use of "tapestry brick" was for the Felsenthal Store (1905); see Morrison, p. 202.

19.
Sullivan, "Suggestions in Artistic Brickwork," 25; see also a similar statement on p. 26.

20.
For a more detailed discussion of Sullivan's color theory and practice as it relates to the treatises of Chevreul and Rood, to the theories of John Ruskin and John Root, and to the techniques of the Impressionists and Neo-Impressionists, see my article "The Colors of Nature: Sullivan's Polychromy and 19th-Century Color Theory," *Winterthur Portfolio* 20 (Winter 1985): 243–60.

21.
"Chevreul On Color" is the title that appears on Sullivan's 1909 auction list; see *Auction Catalogue of the Household Effects, Library, Oriental Rugs, Paintings, etc. of Mr. Louis Sullivan, the Well-Known Chicago Achitect, November 29, 1909* (Chicago: Williams, Barker and Severn Company, 1909), Burnham Library of The Art Institute of Chicago. Many titles on this list are incomplete and inaccurate, and, in this as with other cases, it cannot be determined which edition Sullivan owned. For a review of the publishing history of M. E. Chevreul's *Law of Simultaneous Contrast of Colors* and the impact of Chevreul's color theory on late nineteenth- and twentieth-century painters, see Faber Birren, "Introduction," *The Principles of Harmony and Contrast of Colors and their Applications to the Arts by M. E. Chevreul* (New York: Reinhold Publishing Company, 1967), pp. 5–37. Ogden N. Rood's *Student Textbook of Modern Chromatics* does not appear on Sullivan's auction list. Whether or not he actually owned this text is of little importance since visual analysis of his color combinations and their naturalistic effects provides sufficient evidence for establishing his familiarity with Rood's color theory. In these color compositions Sullivan was likely assisted by his friend and artistic collaborator, Louis J. Millet.

22.
For discussions of Impressionist and Neo-Impressionist techniques and theories, see Richard A. Shiff, *Cézanne and the End of Impressionism: A Study of the Theory, Technique, and Critical Evaluation of Modern Art* (Chicago: University of Chicago Press, 1985), esp. "Part One—The End of Impressionism"; and William I. Homer, *Seurat and the Science of Painting* (Cambridge, Mass.: The MIT Press, 1964).

23.
Sullivan, "Suggestions in Artistic Brickwork," 26. Sullivan also compared the naturalistic polychromatic effects of the Transportation Building with landscape painting. In these elevations Sullivan combined up to thirty hues of red, blue, yellow, and green in delicately interweaving stenciled fresco patterns. See Adler and Sullivan, "Transportation Building" (25 February 1893) in *A Week at the Fair* (Chicago: Rand, McNally & Co., 1893), pp. 43–48.

24.
Carl K. Bennett, "A Bank Built for Farmers," *The Craftsman* 15 (November 1908): 184; this description was repeated in "Louis Sullivan, 'The First American Architect,'" *Current Literature* 52 (June 1912): 706. Tallmadge made a similar allusion to transient Impressionist effects when he observed, "The photographs, though, lack the color and motion that invest the original. . . . The depth of these colors and a total absence of white give the building a certain richness and a prismatic lustre" ("The Farmers' and Merchants' Bank of Columbus," 63). Finally, an oil painting presently located at the National Farmers' Bank in Owatonna, painted by Albert Fleury in 1912, represents the exterior of this bank aglow with an Impressionist palette of reds and greens.

The problem of matching the faded brick in renovations of or modern additions to the banks has been addressed by present-day renovators; see, for example, a discussion of additions to the Farmers and Merchants Union Bank in Columbus, Wisconsin, "Unusual Building was Mr. Wheeler's Dream," *The Columbus Journal-Republican: Farmers and Union Bank 100th Anniversary Edition: 1861–1961* (31 August 1961), n.p.

25.
See Sullivan's description of the decorative scheme of the interior of the main auditorium of the Auditorium Building in *Industrial Chicago*, II (Chicago: Goodspeed Publishing Co., 1891), pp. 490–91; rpt. in Paul, "Appendix," *Louis Sullivan*, pp. 143–46. For the Stock Exchange Trading Room, see John Vinci, *The Art Institute of Chicago: The Stock Exchange Trading Room* (Chicago: The Art Institute of Chicago, 1977).

26.
Sullivan, letter to Carl K. Bennett, 1 April 1908; rpt.: Robert R. Warn, "Part I: Bennett & Sullivan, Client & Creator," *The Prairie School Review* 10 (Third Quarter 1973): 7.

27.
For a discussion of Sullivan's adherence to Richard Wagner's theories of synaesthesia for the production of the total work of art (or in Wagner's popular nineteenth-century term, the *Gesamkunstwerke*), see my article, "The Colors of Nature," 247–52, 257–60.

28.
The National Farmers' Bank is the only remaining example of what Sullivan considered to be a finished bank interior. Some interiors remained unfinished due to limited building budgets or temporary postponements that became permanent. But Sullivan considered his bank interiors complete only when frescoed stencil patterns (and/or figurative landscape paintings) were affixed to "clerestory" walls. See, for example, a description of the incomplete state of the interior of the Peoples Savings and Loan Association in "The Peoples Savings and Loan Association Opening," *The Sidney Daily News* 28 (30 May 1918): 26(?). Tallmadge also made it clear that this

bank's stark interior was only a temporary condition due to the World War I economy; "The Peoples Savings and Loan Association Building of Sidney, Ohio," *The American Architect* 114 (25 October 1918): 480.

29.
See Sullivan, "The Tall Office Building Artistically Considered," 207–8. Sullivan repeated the aphorism "form follows function" in connection with the banks in his article, "Lighting the Peoples Savings Bank," *Illuminating Engineer* 6 (February 1912): 635.

30.
Sullivan attended the French academic institution, the Ecole des Beaux-Arts, from 1874 to 1875. For a discussion of academic methods of composition, see David Van Zanten, "Architectural Composition at the Ecole des Beaux-Arts from Charles Percier to Charles Garnier," in *Architecture of the Ecole des Beaux-Arts,* ed. Arthur Drexler (New York: Museum of Modern Art, 1977).

31.
Just as Sullivan provided a standardized solution for designing the skyscraper, so his logical method of designing the open rural bank plan became a norm for Prairie School architects. For Elmslie and Purcell's development of this rural bank type, see David Gebhard, "William Gray Purcell and George Grant Elmslie and the Early Progressive Movement in American Architecture from 1900 to 1920," Ph.D. Dissertation University of Minnesota, 1957; and for Parker N. Berry's version of the Sullivanian rural bank, see Donald L. Hoffmann, "The Brief Career of a Sullivan Apprentice: Parker N. Berry," *The Prairie School Review* 4 (First Quarter 1967): 8–9. On the basis of Severens's argument in

"The Reunion of Louis Sullivan and Frank Lloyd Wright," we can assume that the influence between Sullivan and Wright in designing the small rural bank was a mutual and often dialectical one. For additional references to Prairie School bank designs, see note 1 in introduction and Alan K. Lathrop, "The Prairie School Bank: Patron and Architect," in *Prairie School Architecture in Minnesota, Iowa, Wisconsin* (exhibition catalogue; St. Paul: Minnesota Museum of Art, 1982), pp. 55–68.

32.
Sullivan defined the "democratic plan" in "Lighting the Peoples Savings Bank"; see note 29 above. This article was reprinted in *The Bankers Magazine* (1912). Lathrop quotes from a 1918 letter written by Sullivan to a "prospective bank client" in which he outlines his rationalist procedures for designing the practical features of a bank ("The Prairie Bank," p. 56; source of this letter is not provided). Sullivan's idea of the "democratic" plan was further popularized in the review, "Peoples Savings and Loan Association Opening," *Sidney Daily News,* 26.

33.
Sullivan, "Lighting the Peoples Savings Bank," 632.

34.
Ibid.

35.
Schuyler, "The Peoples Savings Bank," *The Architectural Record* 31 (January 1912): 55.

36.
Sullivan, "Peoples Savings Bank," 633, 635. In his review of this bank, Schuyler expanded the metaphor of the pagan temple in discussing the contrast between Sullivan's banks and conventional banks.

37.
See, for example, Schuyler, "The Peoples Savings Bank," 49, 52; Tallmadge, "The Farmers' and Merchants' Bank," 64 (here Tallmadge refers to the "nave" windows Sullivan increasingly perfected in the Grinnell, Sidney, and Columbus banks); Kenneth W. Severens, "Louis Sullivan Builds a Small Town Bank," *AIA Journal* 65 (May 1976): 69.

38.
As early as 1895, Sullivan began to disengage and clarify the botanical and geometric compositional motifs in his designs for ornament; see Sprague, *The Drawings of Sullivan,* p. 7. See also Jordy, "Functionalism as Fact and Symbol," p. 382, n. 27, for a bibliographic note on the modernist criticism against Sullivan's ornament. Jordy continues to connect what appeared as overscaled ornament in the banks with Sullivan's psychological life, see pp. 174–79, a preconception he derived from Bush-Brown, *Louis Sullivan,* pp. 30–31 and Connely, *Louis Sullivan as He Lived,* pp. 260–64. Like Bush-Brown and Connely, Menocal appreciates Sullivan's naturalistic color harmonies, and even though he suggests the symbolic function of Sullivan's color and ornament, he finds no other explanation for the enlargement of ornament than a psychological one. See Menocal, *The Transcendentalist Idea of Louis Sullivan,* pp. 128–45. Robert Venturi attempts to reestablish an appreciation for the relationship between ornament and mass in the bank compositions in *Complexity and Contradiction in Architecture* (New York: Museum of Modern Art, 1966), pp. 62–63. But here, too, Venturi appropriates a black-and-white photograph of the Merchants National

Bank in Grinnell, Iowa, a design generally considered the most dissonant of the banks, to confirm his own aesthetic of ironic, visual contradiction.

39.
For a history of Chicago School pragmatism, see Darnell Rucker, *The Chicago Pragmatists* (Minneapolis: University of Minnesota Press, 1969). John Dewey arrived at the University of Chicago in 1894 to head the Philosophy department. Dewey's teachings were already known in Chicago; he had lectured at Jane Addams's Hull House, founded in 1889; for an overview of the Chicago School pragmatists during the "golden" decade, see Rucker, pp. 3–25.

40.
Sherman Paul has also recognized the impact of Chicago School pragmatism on Sullivan's transcendentalist beliefs; see Paul, *Louis Sullivan,* pp. 62, 98. Sullivan's 1909 auction list includes a 1905 edition of William James's *Principles of Psychology* (1890). James, the so-called "father" of pragmatism, was a strong supporter of the Chicago School; see Rucker, *Chicago Pragmatists,* pp. 3–4.

41.
The following discussion of the basic premises of pragmatism is derived primarily from Rucker, *Chicago Pragmatists,* pp. 5–7, 28–57.

42.
At the time of Sullivan's death, Walter Rice observed that a "remarkable" change in Sullivan's writing style occurred with *Democracy: A Man-Search* (manuscript dated 1907–8; published and edited by Elaine Hodges [Detroit: Wayne University Press], 1961) and in *The Autobiography of an Idea;* see "Louis Sullivan as Author," *The West-*

ern Architect 33 (June 1924): 70–71. In this literary context, *Kindergarten Chats* (1901) is a transitional work.

43.
Bennett, "A Bank Built for Farmers," 183. "What is Architecture: A Study in the American People of Today" is reprinted in *Kindergarten Chats and Other Writings,* pp. 227–41. In 1918 Sullivan provided a local journalist a pragmatist tract in connection with a description of the bank; see "Peoples Savings and Loan Association Opening," *The Sidney Daily News,* 26.

44.
In *Kindergarten Chats* (1901) Sullivan had made the distinction between "democratic" and "feudal" architecture one of the primary "lessons" of the student's reeducation in nature. In letters to the publisher of *The Interstate Architect and Builder,* where *Kindergarten Chats* was originally published as a series in fifty-two weekly editions, Sullivan stated that he intended to address these articles to "the young man" and to "the laity, . . . the people, not for architects"; see "Appendix A," in *Kindergarten Chats and Other Writings,* p. 244.

45.
Sullivan, "What is Architecture," 227; Sullivan had made this symbolic association congruent with a linguistic one in this article and earlier in the 1901 version of *Kindergarten Chats;* rpt. ed. Claude Bragdon, *Kindergarten Chats* (Lawrence, Kansas: 1934), see esp. "The Elements of Architecture," pp. 160–70.

46.
Sullivan, "What is Architecture," 230.

47.
Ibid., 240.

48.
Sullivan, "Lighting the Peoples Savings Bank," 635.

49.
Sullivan, "The Modern Phase of Architecture," a letter to Max Dunning, secretary of the Chicago Architectural Club, read in Cleveland, Ohio, at the 1899 convention of the Architectural League of America and published in the *Inland Architect and News Record* 33 (June 1899): 43; rpt. *The Testament of Stone: Themes of Idealism and Indignation from the Writings of Louis Sullivan,* ed. Maurice English (Evanston: Northwestern University Press, 1963), p. 26.

50.
For example, because Frank Lloyd Wright personally contributed to the debate, scholars have tried to determine what parts of such buildings as the Charnley House (1891) are attributable to Wright while he was an apprentice for Adler and Sullivan between 1889 and 1893; see Severens, "Louis Sullivan and Frank Lloyd Wright," 5–7; Henry-Russell Hitchcock, *In the Nature of Materials: The Buildings of Frank Lloyd Wright (1887–1941)* (New York: Duell, Sloan, and Pearce, 1942), pp. 7–14; and Grant C. Manson, *Frank Lloyd Wright: The Golden Years* (New York: Reinhold Publishing Co., 1958), pp. 33–34.

51.
See Sprague, "The Architectural Ornament of Louis Sullivan and his Chief Draftsmen," and *The Drawings of Louis Sullivan,* pp. 8–10.

52.
The problem of identifying Elmslie's hand in designing the ornament and single arch for the Owatonna bank has long been a subject of scholarly debate. Some scholars agree that Elmslie detailed from Sullivan's sketches the ornament for working drawings; others contend that he actually designed most of it according to Sullivan's own mode. See: David Gebhard, "Louis Sullivan and George Grant Elmslie," *Journal of the Society of Architectural Historians* 19 (May 1960): 62–68; Sprague, "The National Farmers' Bank, Owatonna, Minnesota" 4 (Second Quarter 1967): 5–21; cf. Greengard and Gebhard, "Letter(s) to the Editor," *The Prairie School Review* 4 (Third Quarter 1967): 33–36, where Greengard argued for Sullivan's authorship and his collaborative working procedures.

Elmslie did not raise the issue of authorship until much later, in the 12 June 1936 letter to Wright regarding Wright's review of Morrison's monograph (see note 11 above). Elmslie reacted hostilely to Wright's contention that, among other "later works," the Owatonna bank was "unadulterated Sullivan" and, with the Sidney bank, "the only works in which the master shows himself." Elmslie then claimed authorship for "the working drawings and every last detail of decoration," the single arch motif, and the brick counters with glass above and grilles for tellers. See rpt., "Letters to the Editor," *Journal of the Society of Architectural Historians* 20 (October 1961): 140–41. For further reference to this issue, see also the discussion below of National Farmers' Bank, note 21.

53.
See Hoffmann, "Parker N. Berry," 5–6; and John Zukowsky and Pauline Saliga, *Chicago Architects Design: A Century of Architectural Drawings from the Art Institute of Chicago* (New York: The Art Institute of Chicago and Rizzoli International Publications, Inc., 1982), for their entry on Berry, p. 71. Paul Sprague also attributes to Berry parts of the ornamental reliefs at the Grinnell, Newark, and Sidney banks; see "Sullivan and his Chief Draftsmen," pp. 156–59.

54.
Sullivan met Millet at the Ecole des Beaux-Arts when they were both students there. For a discussion of Millet's career as an architectural decorator and educator, see David Hanks, "Louis J. Millet and the Art Institute of Chicago," *Bulletin of The Art Institute of Chicago* 67 (March–April 1973): 13–19.

55.
Schneider is first known to have worked with Sullivan on the relief decoration for the Auditorium Building when Schneider was employed by James Legge, a plastering contractor. Subsequently Schneider was employed by the Northwestern Terra Cotta Company and then the American Terra Cotta Company. The latter firm manufactured the terra cotta and plaster reliefs for all the banks in which Schneider was a collaborator. (Given the absence of finish and chromatic nuances seen in the other banks, it seems that the terra cotta reliefs for the banks at Cedar Rapids, Algona, and West Lafayette were manufactured by local firms.) For a detailed study of Schneider's career as a clay modeler in Chicago, see Martin W. Reinhart, "Norwegian-born Sculptor, Kristian Schneider: His Essential Contribution to the Development of Louis Sullivan's Ornamental Style," a paper presented to The Norwegian American Life of Chicago Symposium, 23 October 1982 (unpublished ms., Department of Architecture, The Art Institute of Chicago).

According to Crombie Taylor, who discussed this issue with me in March 1985, Sullivan is known to have occasionally modeled terra cotta reliefs in the studios of the American Terra Cotta Company; a letter from a former clay modeler to Taylor verifies these activities. For a technical and historical account of artistic collaborations among manufacturers, artisans, and designers of the decorative arts, see Sharon Darling, *Chicago Ceramics and Glass: An Illustrated History 1871–1933* (Chicago: Chicago Historical Society, 1979).

56.
See Sullivan's discussion of the creative process in "Emotional Architecture as Compared with Intellectual," 192–93. Elmslie also made a similar statement concerning the preeminence of the first notations in the design process; see his article, "The Statics and Dynamics of Architecture," *Western Architect* 19 (January 1913): 24.

Sullivan's theories on the creative process can be compared to his counterparts in the visual arts, the French Symbolist painters and theorists; see Lauren S. Weingarden, "Louis H. Sullivan's Metaphysics of Architecture (1885–1901): Sources and Correspondences with Symbolist Art Theory" (Ph.D. Dissertation, University of Chicago, 1981).

For a theoretical discussion of the Symbolists' descriptions of the creative process, see Richard A. Shiff, "The End of Impressionism: A Study in Theories of Artistic Expression," *Art Quarterly*, n.s. 1 (Autumn 1978): 338–78. For studies of the nineteenth-century romantic tradition in general and, more specifically, the American romantic mainstream to which Sullivan belongs, see Hugh Honour, *Romanticism* (New York: Icon Editions, Harper & Row,

1979) and Barbara Novak, *Nature and Culture: American Landscape and Painting 1825–1875* (New York: Oxford University Press, 1980).

57.
See, for example, Bennett, who wrote, "Everything is of special design and was first put on paper by Mr. Sullivan," in "A Bank Built for Farmers," 185. See also, Millet, "National Farmers' Bank," 249–54; Tallmadge, "Peoples Savings and Loan Association," 478–79; and Anon., "Peoples Savings and Loan Association Opening," *Sidney Daily News*, 26.

58.
For discussions of the Arts and Crafts movement in Chicago, which took root as early as the 1870s, see Sharon Darling, *Chicago Furniture: 1833–1983* (Chicago: Chicago Historical Society, 1984); Darling, *Chicago Ceramics and Glass;* and Brooks, *The Prairie School*, pp. 16–25. For a general history of the Arts and Crafts movement in the United States, see David M. Cathers, *Furniture of the American Arts and Crafts Movement: Stickley and Roycroft Mission Oak* (New York: New American Library, 1981); and Isabelle Anscombe and Charlotte Gere, *Arts and Crafts in Britain and America* (London: Academy Editions, 1978).

59.
Stickley founded *The Craftsman* magazine in 1901.

60.
Sullivan was a member of Elbert Hubbard's Society of Philistines. Hubbard was a Morrisonian follower, who, like Stickley, manufactured and sold Craftsman furniture; see Warn, "Bennett and Sullivan," 8–9. Hubbard's headquarters were in East Aurora,

New York, but Sullivan would have had contact with the Morris followers in Chicago who founded the Chicago Arts and Crafts Society in 1897 and the Industrial Arts Club in 1899; see Brooks, *Prairie School*, p. 19.

61.
Sprague suggests the choice of Craftsman furniture for the Owatonna bank was Sullivan's but that "some of the furniture . . . was specially built in plain oak from designs perhaps by Sullivan but more probably by Elmslie." Sprague adds, "The remaining furniture, also of unadorned oak, was purchased from Gustav Stickley's Craftsman's Guild" ("The National Farmers' Bank," 14).

62.
Bennett, "A Bank Built for Farmers," 184.

63.
See, for example, William Morris, "The Revival of Handicrafts" (1888) and "Architecture and History" (1884) in *The Collected Works of William Morris*, vol. 22, ed. May Morris (London: Longmans, Green and Co., 1915).

64.
Sullivan, "Development of Construction," *The Economist* 55 (24 June 1916): 1252; 56 (1 July 1916): 39–40.

65.
Ibid., 1252.

66.
For local impressions of technological innovations, see the discussion of National Farmers' Bank, note 20, below; discussion of Merchants' National Bank, note 15 below; and "Peoples Savings and Loan Association," note 57 above.

67.
Sullivan, "The Tall Office Building Artistically Considered," 206. See also an explanation of Sullivan's partial use of skeletal steel construction in the banks in the review, "Peoples Savings and Loan Association Opening," *Sidney Daily News*, 26.

68.
Sullivan devised open floor plans for the office spaces of the skyscrapers, allowing tenants to place partitions between steel supports according to individual needs. See Morrison's description for the Wainwright Building (1890) in *Louis Sullivan*, p. 146, and the prospectus brochures for the Stock Exchange Building (1893) and Bayard Building (1897) (Fine Arts Library, Princeton University). Sullivan also designed open floor plans for the Schlesinger-Mayer Store (1899); see Morrison, p. 198.

69.
Sullivan also used double-glazed windows in the skyscrapers as insulation and protection for stained glass in, for example, the Pueblo Opera House (1889–90) and Guaranty Building (1894–95). For a discussion of other technological features that first appeared in the skyscraper, see Lloyd C. Engelbrecht, "Adler and Sullivan's Pueblo Opera House: City Status for a New Town in the Rockies," *Art Bulletin* 67 (June 1985): 284, 287–88.

70.
See Morrison regarding the double window insulation at Owatonna and Grinnell banks, pp. 209, 218.

71.
Ferdinand E. Freytag, architect and preservationist who renovated the Sidney bank, was especially impressed by the easy con-

version of Sullivan's cooling system to modern technology (my conversation with Freytag took place in June 1984). Freytag's first-hand experience confirms Morrison's observation that "the mechanical equipment of the [Sidney] bank was very advanced, especially in the system of air-conditioning" (see *Louis Sullivan*, p. 223).

72.
Tallmadge, "The Farmers' and Merchants' Bank," 65.

73.
See Bennett, "A Bank Built for Farmers," 176, 183; "Historical Sketches of Peoples Federal Savings and Loan Association" (Sidney, Ohio: [1981]); and remarks by J. Russell Wheeler, president of the Farmers and Merchants Bank, in John Szarkowski, *The Idea of Louis Sullivan* (Minneapolis: University of Minnesota Press, 1956), p. 5.

74.
For a typical statement regarding connections between urban design and civic patriotism in the City Beautiful movement, see Theodore E. Burton, "Civic Betterment," *The American City* I (September 1909): 14. Burton's statement appeared in the first number of *The American City*, a journal of the City Beautiful movement, and can be considered a manifesto of the movement's ideology. For a recent historical overview, see Jon A. Peterson, "The City Beautiful Movement: Forgotten Origins and Lost Meanings," *Journal of Urban Design* 2 (August 1976): 415–34.

75.
Carole Rifkind has made a similar observation in *Main Street: The Face of Urban America* (New York: Harper and Row, 1977), p. 70.

Color Plates

Plate 1
National Farmers' Bank, Owatonna, Min-
nesota, 1906–8. Photo: Crombie Taylor,
FAIA.

Plate 2
National Farmers' Bank, detail of north
elevation. Mural painting by Oskar Gross.
Photo: Crombie Taylor, FAIA.

Plate 3
National Farmers' Bank, detail of arch, north elevation. Photo: Crombie Taylor, FAIA.

Plate 4
National Farmers' Bank, opalescent and stained glass window, south elevation. Photo: Crombie Taylor, FAIA.

Plate 5
Merchants National Bank, Grinnell, Iowa,
1913–15. Photo: Crombie Taylor, FAIA.

Plate 6
Merchants National Bank, detail of architrave relief. Photo: Crombie Taylor, FAIA.

Plate 7
Merchants National Bank, detail of rose window. Photo: Crombie Taylor, FAIA.

Plate 8
**Home Building Association, Newark, Ohio,
1914–15. Detail of mosaic and relief
over main entrance. Photo: Lauren S.
Weingarden.**

Plate 9
**Home Building Association, detail of ceil-
ing fresco. Photo: Richard Nickel, courtesy of Crombie Taylor, FAIA.**

Plate 10
Peoples Savings and Loan Association,
Sidney, Ohio, 1916–18. Photo: Crombie
Taylor, FAIA.

Plate 11
Peoples Savings and Loan Association,
west elevation. Photo: Crombie Taylor,
FAIA.

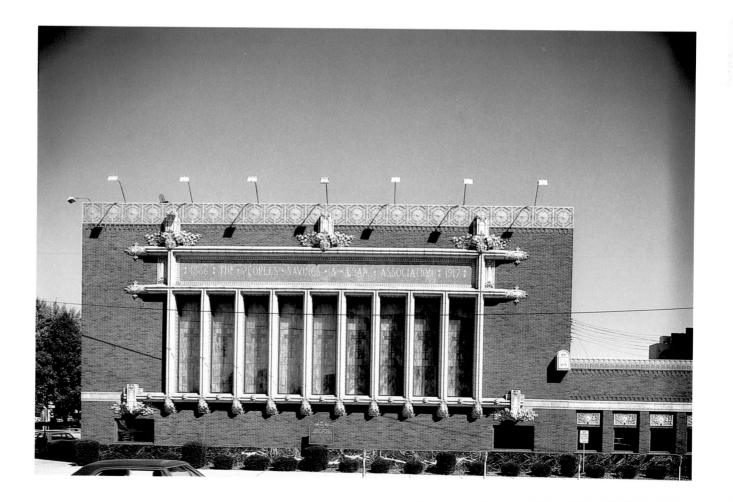

Plate 12
Peoples Savings and Loan Association, detail of mosaic and relief over main entrance. Photo: Lauren S. Weingarden.

Plate 13
Peoples Savings and Loan Association, opalescent and stained glass windows, west elevation. Photo: Crombie Taylor, FAIA.

Plate 14
Farmers and Merchants Union Bank, Co-
lumbus, Wisconsin, 1919–20. Detail of
south elevation. Photo: Crombie Taylor,
FAIA.

Plate 15
Farmers and Merchants Union Bank, view
toward rear. Photo: Crombie Taylor, FAIA.

A Catalogue of the Banks

Introduction

The purpose of the second part of this survey is twofold. First, I treat matters of documentation. To establish dates, costs, and dimensions of each bank I have primarily used local newspapers, historical society archives, bank records, and the collections of Sullivan drawings and memorabilia at the Department of Architecture at The Art Institute of Chicago and the Avery Library of Columbia University. My second purpose in this building survey is to highlight in each bank a different facet of Sullivan's approach to the midwestern rural town bank. Because I want to give a comprehensive review of each bank, some fragmentation and repetition inevitably occur in these discussions. However, I have chosen this method as yet another way to restore the integrity of each bank both as a unique design and as part of a norm.

The Owatonna bank is the most comprehensively documented of Sullivan's banks. It is also Sullivan's most complete realization of a naturalistic interior scheme. This first example provides a model for collecting facts on the banks' building histories and for determining the extent to which Sullivan achieved complete works of art in the other banks. By contrast, in his next bank Sullivan faced financial restrictions that limited his overall decorative program. But for the Cedar Rapids bank Sullivan first fully defined the democratic plan. In the next two commissions, for the Algona Land and Loan Office and the West Lafayette bank, Sullivan encountered more severely limited budgets. These two designs show how Sullivan reduced his material means but sustained his theoretical and formal principles to design naturalistic harmonies and democratic plans for even the smallest bank commission.

The next four designs best illustrate how Sullivan composed the rural town bank as a self-contained entity and as a response to the given built environment. The Newark and Grinnell banks, so different from one another in formal terms, are related by Sullivan's ability to establish reciprocity between the interior and exterior of the bank and between the bank and its surroundings. The Grinnell bank is also historically important because we still have Sullivan's first, on-site sketches, the kind of studies that resulted in the final designs for each bank project. At the site of the Sidney bank, Sullivan encountered two prominent civic monuments with different revival styles, a condition that forced him to reassert the didactic functions of his ornament in shaping a new American style. This building also offers a rare opportunity to study a bank that has remained virtually unchanged. Sullivan again redefined local architectural styles in his design for the Columbus bank; but he also extended the social functions of the democratic plan to accommodate his client's community activities, activities that converged with his own pragmatist ideals for social progress.

N.E. corner Broadway and Cedar Street

Owatonna, Minnesota

Dates

Sullivan working on plans: 20 October 1906[1]

Final plans: 15 January 1907

Sullivan working on interior decoration:

1 April 1908 (letter to Bennett)

Official opening: 16 July 1908

Remodeling: 1929, 1940, 1957–58, 1976 (annex)

Renovation: 1982–83 (main block)

National Register of Historic Landmarks: 1976

Dimensions

68 × 68 feet (main block)

Cost

$125,000

In 1912 Montgomery Schuyler reported that the National Farmers' Bank in Owatonna, Minnesota, had become "the Mecca of architectural pilgrimage [attracting] twenty-five strangers a day."[2] With the completion of this bank in 1908, Sullivan began his second career as a preeminent designer of a rural commercial building type. The initial popular and professional esteem for the National Farmers' Bank has endured: it has been the most consistently praised and thoroughly documented of all Sullivan's banks. Such extensive documentation allows us to reconstruct with relative accuracy the major issues of this commission: the clients' demands; the relation of the bank to its site; Sullivan's building and artistic techniques; and popular responses to the completed work.[3] As a result, the Owatonna bank provides a prototype for reconstructing the building histories of subsequent banks.

There are several reasons for ongoing acclaim for and historical attention to this bank. First, Sullivan demonstrated to his contemporaries how to extend his theories and methods of design from the urban skyscraper to the rural bank. With the National Farmers' Bank, Sullivan provided a model for a new building type that he and his Prairie School followers continued to develop and refine. Another reason is that Sullivan's client, Carl K. Bennett, provided the artistic, emotional, and financial support for Sullivan to realize what both artist and client considered a complete work of art.[4]

Bennett, the vice-president of the bank founded by his father in 1873, established both a professional relationship and a personal friendship with Sullivan that lasted from 1906 until 1917. Sullivan frequently visited Owatonna and stayed with the Bennett family while the bank was being built. On such occa   ' with Bennett a love for music and art and an aesthetic and ideological involvement with the American Arts and Crafts movement. Bennett further encouraged Sullivan to realize his artistic objectives by personally convincing the bank's board of directors to invest nearly $125,000 in total building costs.[5] Sullivan paid tribute to his patron's dedication when he wrote to Bennett:

My whole Spring is wrapped up just now in the study of color and out of doors for the sake of your bank decorations . . . I want a color symphony and I am pretty sure I am going to get it . . . . There has never been in my entire career such an opportunity for a color tone poem as your bank interior plainly puts before me.[6]

But Sullivan did much more than merely fulfill his own aesthetic ideals. He reciprocated Bennett's artistic patronage by meeting the expectations of both Bennett and his colleagues. He designed for them a building that depicts their sound business practices, their independent rural spirit, and their progressive social and civic responsibilities.[7] Sullivan's subsequent clients recognized this achievement and commissioned him to make similar architectural statements about their public image.

Upon receiving the Owatonna commission, Sullivan immediately faced the kinds of programmatic restrictions and aesthetic opposition that he would encounter in later bank projects. Bennett and the other members of the building committee so thoroughly defined their practical needs that they devised a layout for their new bank building even before they thought about a designer. Like their counterparts in both rural and urban centers, these bankers at first envisioned a traditional temple form as the outer shell for their otherwise unique scheme. But just before they began their official search, Bennett read in *The Craftsman* about Sullivan's innovative and practical building designs and his democratic ideals for a new American architecture.[8] Bennett contacted Sullivan in Chicago and commissioned him to design a new building as "an adequate expression of the character of their [banking] business." However, Bennett and Sullivan could not immediately begin their project; some members of the building committee continued to equate the bank as a building type with the classical temple form. Bennett finally persuaded these members that the temple form was not necessarily expressive of nor practical for a bank. He argued that it was especially inappropriate for a bank that prided itself on representing a prosperous dairy-farming community.

When Sullivan arrived in Owatonna in late September or early October 1906, the building committee presented him with their layout.[9] The committee stipulated that the building site, which was larger than necessary for banking facilities, should be divided into a 68 by 68 foot square corner for a "monumental bank building." The remainder of the lot was to be used for an attached two-story rental annex. Sullivan designed distinctive but related compositions for each of these facilities.

Sullivan first conceived the main bank building and the annex as visual analogues. He originally designed the facades of the two street elevations of the main structure with a three-arch motif. Although renderings for this preliminary scheme no longer exist, the arrangement was probably similar to the one he would later propose for the facade of the Farmers and Merchants Union Bank (1919; figure 53). In the Owatonna scheme such an arcade would be echoed in eight arches on the second story of the attached wing. Sullivan composed the annex with the formula he had devised for urban commercial building types, making the annex a scaled-down version of a skyscraper. He ordered a variety of spaces into a U-shaped rectangular mass with a three-part elevation: a "base" for two ground-story shops, a window arcade for fifteen uniform office "cells," and a modified cornice as a formal terminus.[10] He also subordinated the annex's proportions, composition, and color scheme to those of the main block and the surrounding commercial and civic buildings (figures 6, 7).

These original solutions suggest that during his initial visit to Owatonna, Sullivan conceived both the main bank block and the adjacent annex facade as revisions of the round-arched eclectic styles that prevail in Owatonna's business and civic centers. Many of the town's commercial facades are characterized by round-arched Italianate and classical revival styles. Sullivan seems to have particularly responded to the pilaster and arch motif of the Renaissance revival structure opposite the bank on the northwest corner of Broadway and Cedar Street. The Steele County courthouse and Owatonna town hall, which make up the town's civic center, are on axis with and face the bank across Central Park. From these more ponderous Romanesque revival style buildings, Sullivan derived a monumental scale for the bank.[11]

When Sullivan returned to Chicago, he completed the final bank design.[12] He replaced the triple-arch elevations with a single semicircular arch inscribed in a square, a composition he reworked from his earlier repertoire of reductivist designs. Here he used the elemental arch form to depict, by way of contrasts, spatial and structural components of the design. With these broad semicircles he enframed the deep-set stained glass windows within the two 45-foot-high brick walls and contrasted the wide open spans with a massive, closed stone base. By contrasting solids and voids, Sullivan signaled that the inner banking hall is illuminated more expansively than the subordinate spaces. To introduce more light to these surrounding areas, Sullivan penetrated the base with smaller,

precisely cut rectangular windows. He further defined the foundation and the superstructure it supports by contrasting the smoothly finished and uniformly colored sandstone base with the lively, textured, rough-cut tinted pressed brick walls above.[13]

To make the simple cube monumental, Sullivan extended similar abstract formal relationships to other parts of the exterior of the main block. He restated the three-part formula for the annex with more reductivist, three-dimensional forms. In this grander scheme, Sullivan designed a boldly overhanging cornice that adds to the overall monumentality of the block. But he also paid close attention to details. He employed bands of ornamental terra cotta reliefs and brickwork patterns to harmonize the cornice with the cube. Schuyler particularly admired Sullivan's sculptural modulation of the cornice. He observed how it fulfilled an aesthetic demand for "finish."[14] That is, Schuyler believed that the gradations of lights and shadows provided the necessary transitions between vertical and horizontal planes to relieve the geometric severity of the contours and masses.

Sullivan's polychromatic treatment of the Owatonna bank exterior remains one of its most distinguishing and innovative features (plate 1). Using tinted brick as a surfacing material, Sullivan mixed a broad range of individually pigmented bricks to suggest a painterly, impressionistic canvas. He used a subordinate range of blue-green decorative materials to enhance and ensure the "reddish lustre" emitted from these surfaces. He enframed the rectilinear contours of the elevations with a band of dominantly blue and green mosaics, then intensified the general chromatic brilliance of this framework with contrasting reddish-brown, yellow, and white tiles. Sullivan repeated a similar color scheme in the monumental terra cotta relief medallions that anchor the upper four corners of the elevations. Finally, he restated Chevreul's law of simultaneous contrast of colors from a more distant prospect; when viewed from the exterior, the individual colors of the stained glass windows blend into a dominantly blue-green hue.

For the interior, Sullivan devised a color composition in which either cool or warm green tones prevail, depending on outdoor light (plates 2–4). In a letter to Bennett, dated 1 April 1908, Sullivan explained that in the Owatonna bank he wanted to recreate with color the natural and musical effects of "early spring and autumn." He confided that he would count on Louis J. Millet, who he called "the best chorus master . . . the greatest colorist extant," to help him realize his artistic endeavor.[15] Sullivan and Millet collaborated to translate Sullivan's two-dimensional ornamental fresco patterns into delicate chromatic harmonies. They combined 240 shades of contrasting and analogous hues of yellow, red-orange, and green. These fresco patterns determine dominant golden-brown and green hues that shift from orange to blue tints with the changing conditions of natural light. Sullivan and Millet employed a similar combination of yellow, red-orange, and green in the gilded and glazed terra cotta reliefs that border the frescoes, the stained glass windows and mural paintings of the arches opposite the south and west window arches,[16] and the electroliers of the main banking hall.

Sullivan also selected interior surfacing materials to produce color harmonies by reflection and optical blending of the complementary hues of red and green. This chromatic arrangement alternates from the green tile floor, to the red Roman brick wainscotting, and back to green terra cotta relief capping. The "Craftsman finish" of "a soft brown tone [with] a subtle undertone of green"[17] takes part in the subtle reflections of colored light. But it is the opalescent glass windows, tinted with blue-violet and orange-ochre patterns of shields and scrolls, that guarantee the overall "warm, rich, and glowing effect."[18] When daylight filters through these expansive arched windows and the skylight over the main banking hall, the colored light scintillates on the enveloping walls and polychromed surfaces to reproduce the flickering, shifting illumination of a forest interior.

In the Owatonna bank interior Sullivan did not fully realize the more emphatic visual directives and overt symbolism of the democratic plan. Nevertheless, he achieved the dramatic spatial effects intrinsic to such a scheme.[19] A local newspaper reporter observed that one was "hardly prepar[ed]" for the passage from the vestibule into the main banking room, where "the grandeur and beauty [of the] large airy expanse excites wonder."[20] Sullivan created this impression of an open, spacious interior by compressing a smaller cube within a larger one. But to make the inner banking hall monumental, he raised the height of the smaller cube and filled it with light (figures 8–11).

Sullivan articulated each interior space in relation to the banking activities (figures 8, 9, 12). As he would in the later banks, he placed the vaults on axis with the entrance; however, he screened the vaults behind the ornamental cast-iron relief wickets of the tellers' cages. This arrangement, predetermined by his clients, circumvented the overt symbolism of the democratic plan in which the vaults are in full view. But Sullivan brought forth the democratic functions of this bank in other ways. He distributed natural light throughout the subordinate spaces that surround and open onto the central banking hall. In addition, he called

6
National Farmers' Bank, Owatonna, Minnesota, 1906–8. Photo: Henry Fuermann, Chicago Architectural Photographing Co.

7
National Farmers' Bank, view of office and warehouse annex. Photo: Henry Fuermann, Chicago Architectural Photographing Co.

8
National Farmers' Bank, banking room.
Photo: Henry Fuermann, Chicago Architectural Photographing Co.

9
National Farmers' Bank, banking room, view toward tellers' space. Photo: Henry Fuermann, Chicago Architectural Photographing Co.

10
National Farmers' Bank, banking room, view toward entrance from officers' platform. Photo: Henry Fuermann, Chicago Architectural Photographing Co.

11
National Farmers' Bank, cross section through banking room. Reprinted from *Architectural Record* 24 (October 1908): 250.

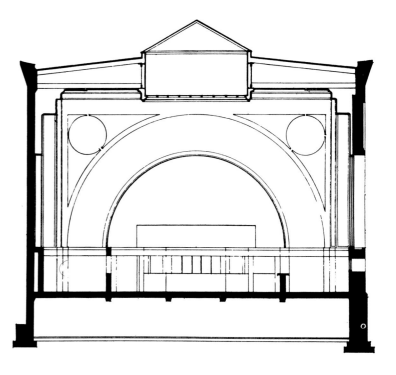

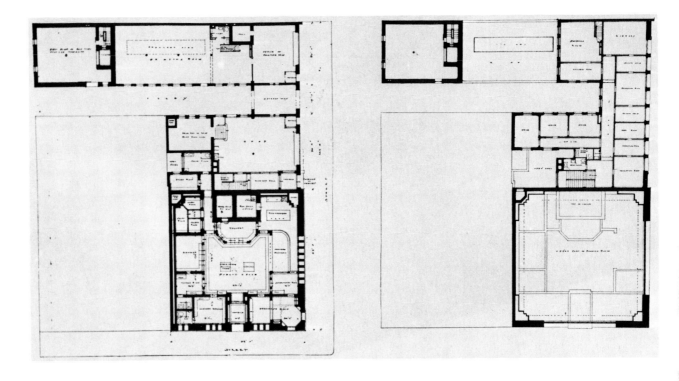

12
**National Farmers' Bank, plans of main
floor and upper floor. Reprinted from *Architectural Record* 24 (October 1908): 251.**

13
National Farmers' Bank, President's
Room. Photo: Henry Fuermann, Chicago
Architectural Photographing Co.

attention to the status of the farmer within this rural village. He gave equally prominent spaces to the Farmers' Exchange Room and the President's Room (figure 13), located at either side of the entrance vestibule.

The layout and design for the National Farmers' Bank make this building a transitional work. It is difficult to speculate whether Sullivan would have realized his democratic plan if he had not been limited by his clients' demands.[21] However, the relationship of ornament to mass on the exterior elevations does place this bank in relation to Sullivan's earlier and later works. On the one hand, Sullivan subordinated his organic mode of ornament to the simple geometric contours of the mass-composition, an arrangement that makes this design continuous with the larger urban structures. On the other hand, he increased the scale of the ornament so that the organic imagery begins to compete with the geometric simplicity of the cube. In the smaller banks that followed, Sullivan exploited this contrast between organic ornament and reductivist mass. He composed a more complementary relationship to produce a surface tension and dynamic balance between the two primary elements of his symbolic representation.

The local press in Owatonna paid close attention to the progress of the National Farmers' Bank. When the bank was completed, Henry Fuermann arrived to take a photographic survey of the bank for the *Architectural Record*. This event gives a good indication of the residents' pride in the new structure; a journalist suggested that when the newspaper obtained Fuermann's photographs, its "readers could send them to their friends all over the country."[22] The opening ceremony also indicates that the bank officials were pleased with the results of the project; for this event they chose evening hours to display the interior in the most dramatic

way—illuminated by the golden glow of the electroliers. While this ambience stirred emotional responses among the guests, reporters were also attuned to the bank's "progressive" appearance. One observer admired it as a "modern," "model bank" constructed entirely with "fireproof materials, steel, concrete, brick and tile. . . . It is on a concrete foundation." This same reporter added, "Even the window casings are of steel. The only parts of wood in the entire bank are the doors, settees, chairs, desks, and tables."[23] Contemporary viewers also associated the "massive," "solid" appearance with the actual function of a bank, which validated Bennett's efforts to find an image to represent the bank as a place of safekeeping.

Bennett understood Sullivan's architectural imagery to be open-ended, offering poetic metaphors as well as more literal references with which a banker could shape his own public image. In 1911 he wrote to Sullivan, "I have often likened your work to that of the great musicians or poets, and have thought of ourselves as though we possessed exclusively one of the symphonies of Beethoven."[24] In his public statements Bennett used Sullivan's innovative design to exemplify his twofold endeavor for civic leadership and financial success. In this regard, he claimed that he and his bank colleagues had demanded "an adequate expression of the character of their business in the form of a simple, dignified and beautiful building due to themselves and due to their patrons." Furthermore, "they believed that a beautiful business house would be its own reward and that it would pay from the financial point of view in increased business."[25]

When Bennett commissioned Sullivan to design the Owatonna bank, he joined the architect in building for posterity. Bennett predicted in 1908 that "the building will increase in value as years go by and will be as adequate for use and as fresh and inspiring in its beauty one hundred years from now as it is today."[26] Bennett was at least partially right. Today the National Farmers' Bank is one of the few banks that has undergone sympathetic adaptation to modern banking needs while retaining the integrity of the original design.

Notes

1.
American Contractor, 20 October 1906; cited by David P. Bowers in "The National Farmers' Bank of Owatonna: A Documentation Project for the Northwestern Bank of Owatonna" (1976; unpublished, unpaginated ms. located in the [now Northwestern] bank archives); see "Design and Construction of National Farmers' Bank."

2.
Schuyler, "The Peoples Savings Bank of Cedar Rapids, Iowa," 47.

3.
See: Bowers, "Documentation Project"; Warn, "Part I: Bennett & Sullivan, Client & Creator," *The Prairie School Review* 10 (Third Quarter 1973): 5–15 and "Part II: Louis H. Sullivan, '. . . an air of finality,' " *Prairie School Review* 10 (Fourth Quarter 1973): 5–19; Sprague, "The National Farmers' Bank," 5–21; and Morrison, *Louis Sullivan,* pp. 207–10. See also the bank pamphlet, "An Architectural Symphony: Northwestern National Bank of Owatonna Presents a Pictorial History of Architect Louis H. Sullivan's National Farmers Bank Building Owatonna, Minnesota."

4.
The following discussion of Bennett's relationship with Sullivan is taken from Warn's articles and Bowers's "Documentation Project."

5.
Bowers estimated this amount by adding architect's fees and banking fixtures to what Bennett quoted—$80,000 for bank structure and $30,000 for annex; see Bowers, "Documentation Project," section on "Design and Construction."

6.
Warn, "Bennett & Sullivan," 7.

7.
For discussion of Bennett's activities as a civic leader in Owatonna, see Warn, "Louis H. Sullivan," 6–7; and Bowers, "Documentation Project." For Bennett's statements concerning associations he made between progressive architecture and progressive banking and civic leadership, see his "A Bank Built for Farmers," 176–85 and the "Editor's Note" that precedes it. Cf. Bennett's statements with articles that appeared in *The American City,* a City Beautiful journal first published in 1909; see, for example, T. E. Burton, "Civic Betterment," *The American City* I (September 1909): 14.

Louis J. Millet corroborated Bennett's associations between progressive banking, rural independence, and innovative architecture. Millet wrote that the Owatonna bankers set an example for their urban counterparts to follow "a new path . . . a lesson in simplicity and directness." See Millet, "The National Farmers' Bank of Owatonna," 249–50, 252.

8.
Bennett, "A Bank Built for Farmers," 183; cf. Sullivan, "The Possibility of a New Architectural Style," *The Craftsman* 8 (June 1905): 336–38; "Form and Function Artistically Considered," *The Craftsman* 8 (July 1905): 453–58; "What is Architecture? A Study in the American People of Today," *The Craftsman* 10 (May–June 1906): 145–49, 352–58, 507–13.

9.
See Bowers, "Documentation Project," section on "Design and Construction." There is a small warehouse at the rear of

the lot forming an L-shaped court, like the light courts of the skyscrapers.

10.
Here Sullivan transformed the skyscraper's projecting cornice into a narrow band of ornamental relief.

In a conversation with me in March 1985, Crombie Taylor observed that the top three feet of brickwork have been removed from the annex building. This has resulted in disproportion in scale and a break in the horizontal band originally connecting the annex and main bank.

11.
The Owatonna town hall, dated 1906 in the name plate between the first and second stories, presented a newly built revival style civic building for Sullivan's critical response. Bowers suggests that the original elliptical shape of Central Park inspired Sullivan's single arch scheme; see "Design and Construction."

12.
Most historians accept Elmslie's claim that it was upon Sullivan's return that he suggested the single-arch motif to Sullivan. He made such a claim in letters to Hugh Morrison (29 May 1931) and to Wright (12 June 1936); see, respectively, Sprague, "The National Farmers' Bank," 10 and *Journal of the Society of Architectural Historians* 20 (October 1961): 140. In the letter to Wright Elmslie took credit for the single arch, for which Morrison also paid him due; see Morrison, *Louis Sullivan,* p. 210; Sprague, "The National Farmers' Bank," 10; Gebhard, "Sullivan and Elmslie," 66; and notes 52 and 57 above.

I would argue that the enframement of a single Richardsonian arch within a cubic mass follows the formula Sullivan had often used much earlier. Two well-known ex-

amples of this scheme are the Getty Tomb (1890) and the Golden Doorway of the Transportation Building (1893). A third lesser-known example is Kehilath Anshe Ma'ariv Synagogue (1890–91). We can conclude that Elmslie simply retrieved what had been Sullivan's own reductivist theme for building types that were not skyscrapers. Gebhard neglected these prototypes when he attributed the broad arch and cube motif of the Owatonna Bank facade to Elmslie, since it is "characteristic of Elmslie's later work"; see "Sullivan and Elmslie," 66. Gebhard further deflected Elmslie's continuity with Sullivan's designs in a later note. He located Elmslie's "source" for the arch within a cube in Harvey Ellis's 1888 design for the Security Bank of Minneapolis; see "Letter to Editor," *Prairie School Review* 4 (Third Quarter 1967): 34–35.

13.
Sullivan mastered this geometric severity and the tectonic relationship between the base and the superstructure in his earlier commercial buildings, such as the Walker Warehouse (1888) and the Wainwright Building (1890).

14.
Schuyler, "The Peoples Savings Bank," 49, 55.

15.
Letter from Sullivan to Bennett reprinted in Warn, "Bennett & Sullivan," 7.

16.
Mural paintings were painted by Oskar Gross; see Morrison, *Louis Sullivan,* p. 209.

17.
Bennett, "A Bank Built for Farmers," 184.

18.
Ibid., 185.

19.
Millet described the interior effects as "psychological"; see "The National Farmers' Bank," 254.

20.
"Farmers Bank has Moved," *The Peoples Press* 32 (17 July 1908): 1.

21.
Bowers, "Documentation Project," section on "Design of National Farmers' Bank."

22.
"Noted Chicago Photographer Here Getting Views of New National Farmers Bank," *Chronicle-Journal,* 13 July 1908, n.p. Reporters also took pride in the fact that Henry Fuermann's brother, Charles, formerly ran a brewery in the town.

23.
See "Farmers Bank has Moved," *The Peoples Press,* 1. According to Bowers, the elevations were constructed with common brick (faced with sandstone at the base) and pressed brick for street elevations (see "Design of National Farmers' Bank"). The arched windows, according to Morrison, are double glazed and hermetically sealed for insulation; see *Louis Sullivan,* p. 209.

24.
Bennett's letter to Sullivan cited from Warn, "Louis H. Sullivan," 6.

25.
Bennett, "A Bank Built for Farmers," 176.

26.
Ibid., 185.

S.W. corner First Street and Third Avenue, S.W.

Cedar Rapids, Iowa

Dates

First plans, call for contractors: 9 August 1909

Contractors' bids rejected: 1 December 1909

Basement plans complete; new bids received: 10 June 1910

Revised working drawings: 14 July 1910

Revised plans accepted: 29 August 1910

Foundation construction begun: July/August [?] 1910

Official opening: 7 September 1911

Remodeling: first addition, 1951; second addition and remodeling, 1966;

remodeling and addition of adjacent four-story building, 1975

National Register of Historic Landmarks: 1978

Dimensions

50 × 90 feet; main banking room 25 × 50 feet

Cost

$62,677

The Peoples Savings Bank is the second of five buildings Sullivan designed for small towns and villages in Iowa between 1909 and 1914. Of these projects, two were designed as banks and one for a related building type, a land and loan office.[1] The conditions of the Cedar Rapids project were just the opposite of those that guaranteed Sullivan's overall success with the Owatonna bank commission.[2] The Peoples Savings Bank commission involved a limited building budget and an indecisive building committee. Both factors caused delays that seem typical of Sullivan's major projects during these years.[3]

Early in 1909 the bank's building committee invited Sullivan to submit plans for a new building.[4] To better scrutinize the practicality of the plan, the committee had a full-scale layout of this first scheme arranged on the floor of the old Cedar Rapids auditorium. After accepting the plan, the committee called for bidders in August 1909 while setting a $42,500 limit on construction costs. On December 1 the committee rejected all bids because cost estimates exceeded this limit; it then suspended negotiations with the architect and contractors. At some point between January and June 1910, the committee asked Sullivan to submit revised plans, for which new bids were obtained. Sullivan's working drawings, dated 14 July 1910 (figures 14–17), were approved in August. At last, on 7 September 1911, the new building officially opened. Sullivan had complied with the limits set by the building committee; the final cost of the land, building, vaults, furniture, boulevard lights, and sidewalks was $62,677.

It seems likely that the building committee commissioned Sullivan because practical concerns outweighed aesthetic considerations. This assumption is substantiated by a letter dated 29 September 1910 from F. H. Shaver, the bank's vice-president, to John D. Van Allen, a businessman from Clinton, Iowa.[5] Shaver recommended Sullivan to Van Allen on the basis of his functional plans and because his designs increased the bank's advertising value. Shaver also pointed out that Sullivan provided additional features—superior skills and worldly fame—at no extra cost.

Shaver's reasons for endorsing Sullivan are important for understanding how the bank's recent history in part determined Sullivan's final scheme. Established in 1900, the Peoples Savings Bank had neither the resources nor the prestige of the twenty-eight-year-old National Farmers' Bank. Furthermore, local businessmen founded the bank to serve the mercantile community of the newly developed west side, an area geographically and economically distinct from the older downtown commercial district.

Paradoxically, the bank's financial restrictions seem to have renewed Sullivan's expertise both as an innovative functionalist planner and as an artistic modeler of monumental, simple forms. In the Peoples Savings Bank, Sullivan realized for the first time what he called the "democratic" plan. He enclosed this plan in reductivist masses that directly represent the purposeful arrangement of interior spaces. With these solutions Sullivan visually restated his precept for making unadorned buildings "comely in the nude,"[6] a precept he had exemplified earlier in his design for the Walker Warehouse (1888).

Schuyler's 1912 review of the Peoples Savings Bank extols the integrity of Sullivan's design. Schuyler used Sullivan's organic-mechanistic metaphor "form follows function" to describe in detail Sullivan's mastery of the open plan. He also applied Sullivan's credo as a criteria for evaluating what he regarded as the most important lesson to be learned from the design as a whole: the organic integrity of the exterior massing and interior layout (figures 14–18).[7]

Schuyler's own aesthetic biases nevertheless caused him to miss other achievements Sullivan attained in the exterior of this bank. His comments suggest that he was unaware of the material limitations and the context that shaped Sullivan's final design. For one thing, Schuyler criticized the "shocking starkness" of the exterior. He regretted the absence of what he called "finish" in the elevations; that is, the sculptural and textural modulation between reductivist masses and between solids and voids. These were the very formal qualities that he admired in Sullivan's other buildings.[8] Furthermore, Schuyler expanded the metaphorical associations of "form follows function" to the bank's exterior appearance—he compared the bank to a medieval "keep," signifying its function as a place of safekeeping.[9] Focusing on these more literal associations, he overlooked the ways in which Sullivan integrated the necessarily austere bank exterior with the town fabric and its commercial activities.

A prestigious corner lot provided Sullivan with an opportunity to exploit a site that mediated the old and new parts of Cedar Rapids.[10] The corner of First Street and Third Avenue is at a major intersection that connects the commercial, civic, and industrial centers of the city. First Street runs parallel to the Cedar Rapids River along the town's industrial north-south axis. Third Avenue is the major east-west axis; it forms a direct link between the west side and the city and county buildings on May Island and, still farther east, the older downtown business district. Monumental residential and religious buildings border its easternmost end. (St. Paul's Methodist Church, a building begun by Sullivan, is located at Third Avenue and Fourteenth Street.) Significantly, early in 1910 the bank's directors contributed $500 in private funds for a new Third Avenue bridge over the Cedar Rapids River. The construction of

14
Peoples Savings Bank, Cedar Rapids,
Iowa, 1909–11. Plan of main floor, 14 July
1910. Ink and colored ink on linen, 69 ×
102.5 cm. © The Art Institute of Chicago.

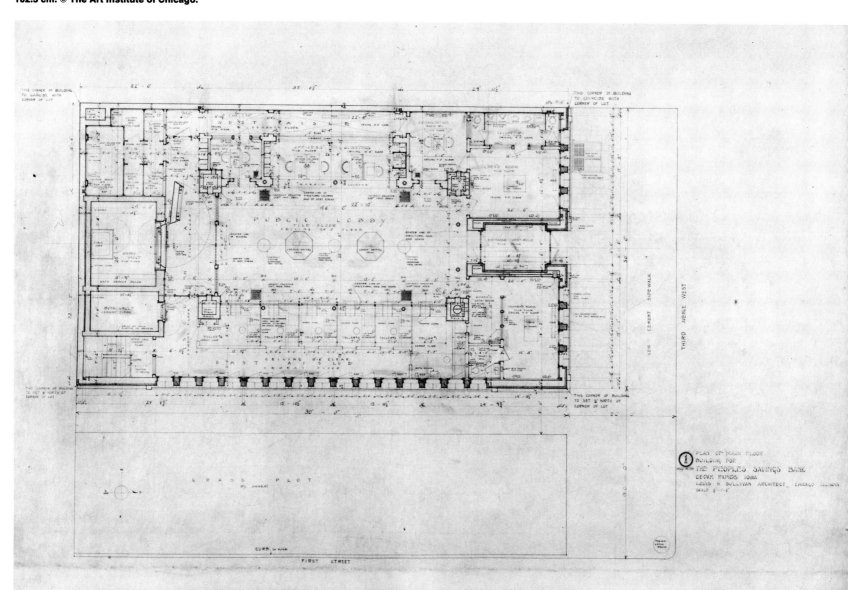

15
Peoples Savings Bank, north and south
elevations, 14 July 1910. Ink and colored
ink on linen, 69 × 102.5 cm. © The Art
Institute of Chicago.

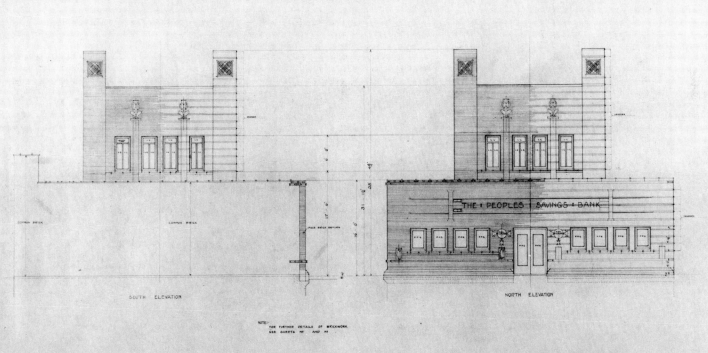

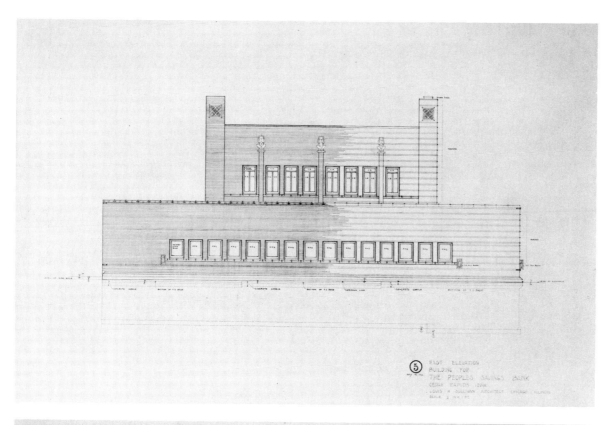

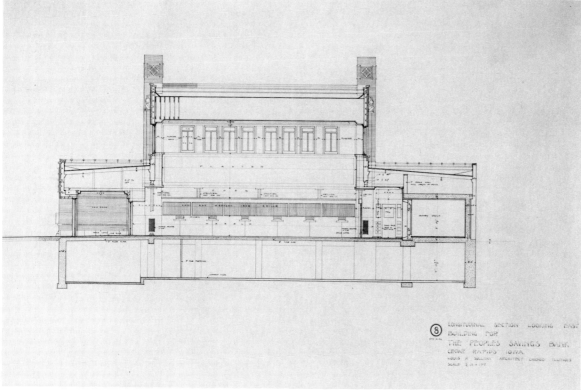

this connector may have encouraged the building committee to recover their project with Sullivan's revised set of plans; the bridge was to be located directly at the intersection that forms the bank's site.

In his final scheme Sullivan accounted for these changing socioeconomic and urban conditions. He composed the exterior elevations as a monumental mass to represent closure from and access to the newly developed commercial section of Cedar Rapids. At the same time, he made this enframement continuous with the adjacent industrial landscape. By emphasizing the verticality of the banking hall setback and its four corner towers, Sullivan visually connected the bank with the grain refinery silos aligning the north-south embankments of the Cedar Rapids River.

Sullivan also devised "artistic" techniques to offset what he considered the building's strictly "mechanical" or utilitarian appearance. As in the Owatonna bank, he faced the exterior with tinted, rough-cut pressed brick and terra cotta reliefs. Here he combined fourteen tones and colors ranging through deep reddish-brown, purple, and grayish-blue and used this tinted clay-like substance to enliven potentially inert masses. Sullivan distributed matching glazed terra cotta ornamental reliefs and sculpture to modulate or to give finish to functional and structural elements in relation to the severely geometric volumes (figures 18, 19). He subdued right-angle contours with relief panels of organic ornament applied to the ventilation towers, the sidewalk street lamps, and the entrance enframement. By affixing guardian winged lions to wall buttresses, he animated the neutral surfaces and contours of the rectangular setback. Sullivan molded terra cotta into horizontal accents to balance the substructure with these vertical dimensions. He gave visual continuity to the whole with the beveled podium, the unbroken string-course below the horizontal window range, and the narrow cornice of finials and inlaid gold leaf.

In the decoration and layout of the bank interior, Sullivan integrated more fully his functionalist, artistic, and symbolic references to democratic architecture (figures 20–24). Schuyler noted that Sullivan intended to make "the interior 'the thing' " in contrast to the exterior, which had been "reduced to . . . its simplest expression." He admired the greater degree of finish Sullivan achieved through "the coordination of allied arts to the whole artistic effect of the interior."[11]

Following Sullivan's verbal exegesis for inverting the "aspects of mystery [and] reserve" associated with the traditional temple-form bank, Schuyler made an analogy between the open interior arrangement and the ideology of democracy.[12] He emphasized the social value of the democratic plan; that is, the overtly functional layout that made visible all banking activities. Schuyler's analogy between forms and concepts helps us see what Sullivan gained in design despite what he lost to a restricted building budget. Such a budget proscribed the decorative grille wickets he used for the Owatonna bank. In this more modest scheme Sullivan used unadorned, vertical bronze slats to separate the tellers from the patrons, a feature that greatly extended vistas within the open interior (figures 21, 22). Sullivan thereby retained, with the most economic means, the lighting and spatial sequences of the Owatonna bank layout.

Drastic and unsympathetic alterations have completely eradicated the dramatic effects of the original interior. But, using the Owatonna interior as a prototype, we can reconceive Sullivan's original spatial, lighting, and chromatic arrangements. Passing from daylight through a low, dark vestibule and into the two-story banking hall, the spectator/user would have

18
Peoples Savings Bank. Reprinted from *Architectural Record* 31 (January 1912): 45.

19
Peoples Savings Bank, detail of lamppost. Reprinted from *Architectural Record* 31 (January 1912): 48.

20
Peoples Savings Bank, view of public lobby toward entrance. Reprinted from *Architectural Record* 31 (January 1912): 50.

21
Peoples Savings Bank, view of public lobby toward vault. Reprinted from *Architectural Record* 31 (January 1912): 53.

22
Peoples Savings Bank, view of public lobby toward tellers' quarters. Reprinted from *Architectural Record* 31 (January 1912): 52.

23
Peoples Savings Bank, view of public lobby toward officers' quarters. Reprinted from *Architectural Record* 31 (January 1912): 51.

24
Peoples Savings Bank, officers' quarters. Reprinted from *Architectural Record* 31 (January 1912): 55.

been awed by a spatial expanse suffused with chromatic mixtures of natural, artificial, and reflected lights (figures 20, 21). *In situ* fragments provide traces of the original color harmony. Dark green veined marble counter tops, green and white floor tiles, and verde antique light fixtures and chandeliers established a dominant color scheme of warm-toned yellowish-green. This scheme was enhanced by a mixture of colored light filtered through the dominantly peacock blue opalescent leaded glass windows in the clerestory, the range of polished plate glass windows behind the tellers' area, and the predominantly yellow skylight over the main banking area.

Soft, warm tones and golden hues also radiated from surrounding surfaces. For example, the shafts of structural steel posts—what Schuyler called "nave piers"—were encased in gilded sheet iron, and their gilded capital reliefs were also polychromed with green and yellow-orange. Four figurative mural paintings rendered with gold backgrounds on the clerestory walls helped to diffuse more subtly the reflected lights (figures 20, 23). Sullivan worked closely with the muralist Allen E. Philbrick, then an instructor at the school of The Art Institute of Chicago, to translate themes of seasonal change into allegories of the bank's purpose. Philbrick painted scenes representing the four seasons and the four branches of Iowa's economy: labor, commerce, industry, and especially agriculture.[13] These figurative representations corresponded to Sullivan's own preoccupations with making visual the cyclical harmony between nature and humanity. Indeed, Sullivan continued these organic associations with the warm brown tones of walnut-shell stained oak wall veneers, wood enframements, and Craftsman-style furniture (figure 24).

Local newspapers recorded the opening celebrations and popular reactions to a novel architectural event. Journalists praised the building for representing "a rare combination of Safety, Utility and Beauty" and commended the bank officials for providing public beauty and utility for the community. In the latter case, reporters noted that the private banking facilities of the Women's Room and assembly rooms would be accessible to the public at all times—even before and after regular banking hours.[14] Local observers associated the bold austerity of the bank's exterior with the bankers' discriminating tastes and practicality, and associated the functional layout with their humanitarian concerns for both the banking public and employees. They approved of the rich interior decoration as an appropriate statement of "the solidity and wealth that becomes a bank that has advanced from small beginnings to the state of a very large and flourishing institution in a brief period."[15]

Newspaper accounts also reported that the West Side Improvement League of Cedar Rapids (a contingent of the City Beautiful movement) praised the Peoples Savings Bank as an "example of what a live and progressive body of men can do for their town and townsmen."[16] The league's perception of the bank owners as civic leaders is a significant one for evaluating Sullivan's achievements as an image-maker for small midwestern banks and their owners. Their view demonstrates that Sullivan's design strengthened a spirit of competition between the townspeople and their urban counterparts. As one writer boasted, the Peoples Savings Bank served as a "magnificent advertisement for the city, . . . better than anything done in Chicago or New York."[17]

Notes

1.
For Sullivan's Iowa commissions, see Morrison, *Louis Sullivan*, pp. 213–16; Connely, *Louis Sullivan*, pp. 251–52, 254–62; Warn, "Louis H. Sullivan," 6; and Anon., "Cedar Rapids to Have the Most Unique Church in the West," *Evening Gazette* 29 (9 September 1911): 1. For a photographic and descriptive survey of Sullivan's works in Iowa rural towns, see Joseph K. Brown, "Iowa Jewel Boxes of Louis Sullivan," *The Iowan* (August–September 1958): 19–25, 50; photographs by Aaron Siskind and J. K. Brown.

2.
This commission coincides with a series of personal crises Sullivan encountered between 1909 and 1911. For the details of these events, see Connely, *Louis Sullivan*, pp. 234–53; Warn, "Bennett & Sullivan," 13–15, and "Louis H. Sullivan," 6. Warn recounts that Bennett attributed Sullivan's loss of interest in designing rural banks to his psychological and physical debilitations. But the financial problems that beset the Cedar Rapids bank project count as much, if not more, for Sullivan's procrastination.

3.
Sullivan faced similar impasses with the 1910 commission for St. Paul's Methodist Church in Cedar Rapids, a project from which he resigned in 1912 and which George Elmslie completed with his partner William Gray Purcell; see Morrison and Connely above. In 1911 Carl Bennett commissioned Sullivan to design a house, but in the next year Bennett suspended the project because of the excessive costs; see Warn, "Louis H. Sullivan," 9–13.

4.
It is reported that Elmslie worked on these preliminary plans prior to leaving Sullivan's office at the end of 1909; see Gebhard, "Louis Sullivan and George Grant Elmslie," 66.

The following accounts of the bank's building and institutional histories are adapted from its anniversary book written by Ted J. Welch, *Peoples Bank: The First 75 Years* (Cedar Rapids: Peoples Bank and Trust Company, [1975]), pp. 17–23. The bank has also published a commemorative pamphlet, "The Beginning of an Era for The Peoples Savings Bank of Cedar Rapids" (n.d.), which includes reprints of Schuyler, "The Peoples Savings Bank," *Architectural Record* (1912) and "The Peoples Savings Bank," *The Bankers Magazine* (1912). *The Bankers Magazine* article was, in turn, composed of excerpts from Sullivan's article, "Lighting the Peoples Savings Bank" from the *Illuminating Engineer* (1912). For additional information about the local history of the bank, see Mary Zielinski, " 'Jewel Box'—Architectural Gem," *Cedar Rapids Gazette* (9 May 1976).

Chicago firms manufacturing facing materials and decorative work include Chicago Ornamental Iron Company (bronze grilles), Northwestern Terra Cotta Company, and David J. Braun Company (electroliers). Two Minneapolis firms, The Northwestern Marble and Tile Company and Bardwell-Robinson Company (cabinet work), also received contracts for decorative work.

5.
Original letter located in the Architecture Department of The Art Institute of Chicago. Perhaps because of such economic advantages, Van Allen hired Sullivan to design and execute a commercial building between 1913 and 1915.

6.
See Sullivan, "Ornament in Architecture," 187.

7.
Schuyler, "The Peoples Savings Bank," 49, 54.

8.
Ibid., 49–55.

9.
Ibid., 54.

10.
Much of the surrounding townscape exists today as it did when the bank was built. Vintage photographs block out the neighboring buildings, which included a furniture store built in 1909–10 on the bank's property next to their building site; see Welch, *Peoples Bank*, p. 18. That four-story building is now part of the Peoples Bank facilities.

11.
Schuyler, "The Peoples Savings Bank," 49, 54.

12.
Ibid., 54; cf. Sullivan, "Peoples Savings Bank," 632.

13.
Schuyler, "The Peoples Savings Bank," 56; Welch, *Peoples Bank*, p. 22. The iconography and medium of these murals recall a similar integration of architecture and decorative and pictorial arts in the main auditorium of the Auditorium Building.

14.
"The Peoples Bank Building," *Evening Gazette* 29 (9 September 1911): n.p.

15.
"New Bank is Model of Beauty and Convenience," *Evening Gazette* 29 (11 September 1911): 1.

16.
Welch, *Peoples Bank*, p. 22.

17.
"The Peoples Bank Building," *Evening Gazette*, n.p.

N.W. corner Moore and State Streets

Algona, Iowa

Dates

Working drawings: 13 April 1913[1]

Construction begun: May 1913[2]

Completion: Fall 1913[3]

Drawings for proposed alterations and additions (unexecuted): 14 March 1920[4]

Dimensions

22 × 70 feet

Sullivan gained local popularity with the completion of the Peoples Savings Bank in Cedar Rapids, Iowa. His Iowa clients admired his ability to design economical, efficient, and artistic bank buildings.[5] It was probably for this reason that in 1913 a prominent Algona businessman, Henry C. Adams, commissioned Sullivan to design a building for his real estate and loan business. Originally called the Land and Loan Office, this structure may not have been intended to be a bank, as Morrison and later historians assumed.[6] Adams began his financing business in the new quarters to serve the local agricultural community. Seven years later he asked Sullivan to design alterations and an addition for the building. This project was never realized; Adams sold the building in 1921. Since that time, it has been used for a variety of functions and has undergone extensive interior changes.[7]

Just as scholars have identified George Grant Elmslie's hand in parts of the Owatonna bank, they have tried to discern the hand of Parker N. Berry, Sullivan's chief draftsman from 1909 to 1917, in the design for the Algona building (figure 25).[8] What was the extent of Sullivan's involvement with a design for an extremely small, low-budget project? In answering this question and the one of attribution, we should first consider the constraints Sullivan faced during this commission. Then we should compare the Algona design with Berry's other designs for banks.

At the time of the Algona commission and the West Lafayette one that followed, Sullivan's friends observed that he was tired of designing small rural banks; his exhaustion may have been due to the obstacles he encountered in the Cedar Rapids bank commission. Still more frustrating for Sullivan were the economic restrictions that would prevent him from achieving a complete work of art. It seems safe to assume that Sullivan allowed Berry a freer hand in carrying out the details and working drawings of his preliminary sketches and designs for these two banks. Sullivan thus continued with Berry a working relationship that he had established with his previous chief draftsmen. But the historian Donald Hoffmann notes:

Although Sullivan maintained authority over his dwindling staff in the years when Berry worked for him, many projects were the work of the young designer. For a time and with Sullivan's permission, Berry was allowed to pursue his own commissions. The Algona, Iowa, business building for Henry C. Adams . . . bears the Sullivan imprint, but the working drawings are by Berry. Not surprisingly, Berry's independent commissions were similar in type—banks, residences—to what Sullivan was designing at the time.[9]

We can identify two elements in the Algona design that are more consistent with Berry's style and are especially prominent in his presentation drawing for the building (figure 26). First, the recessed rectangular entrance, enframed by urn-topped square piers, forms a portico to the enclosed vestibule. Berry used this same arrangement in his independent bank projects: in 1912 for the Lincoln State Bank, Chicago, and in 1915 for the First State Bank of Manlius, Illinois.[10] This recessed portico works as a spatial transition, but it repeats and thus detracts from a similar function in the vestibule. By contrast, Sullivan used the low, dark vestibule as a dramatic transition between the intense daylight and confusion of the commercial street and the modulated light and order of the bank interior. The low, broad horizontal proportions of the portico also represent a more complete appropriation of the Prairie School idiom, first worked out by Frank Lloyd Wright. Such an assimilation is more characteristic of Berry's work than of Sullivan's.[11]

The pier and lintel system that appears in the Algona design is also more consistent with Berry's style. As seen at the entrance and on the side elevation, this tectonic system has the stouter proportions and outlines of classical architecture. Such classicizing tendencies can also be seen in Berry's independent designs—for example, in his project for the Lincoln State Bank. We can compare these examples with Sullivan's designs for the pier and lintel system in the horizontal window range of the side elevation of the Cedar Rapids bank. There, Sullivan simplified the forms and attenuated the proportions of the vertical supports. These changes are similar to his interpretation of the unbroken piers in the shaft of his skyscraper designs. In later bank designs, Sullivan continued to eliminate classical proportions so as to emphasize instead the abstract primary forms of the pier and lintel, which he grouped with the arch as "the three physical facts, the three symbols, the three letters which constitute the alphabet of our architectural art."[12]

The general mass-composition, layout, and lighting relate to Sullivan's designs for his two earlier banks and, by extension, to his earlier commercial buildings. Hugh Morrison admired the simple, reductivist composition as a direct representation of function. He concluded his brief description by observing: "It is so obvious a direct statement of the problem, that problem was so simple, that it needs little comment."[13] Morrison emphasized the austerity of the functional part of the design, but he overlooked Sullivan's equal mastery for making straightforward representation artistic.

A. N. Rebori's review of the Algona building helps us to discern how Sullivan made a diminutive building monumental and, at the same time, prevented the monumental from becoming monolithic. In "An Architec-

25
Land and Loan Office, Algona, Iowa, 1913–14. Reprinted from *Architectural Record* 39 (May 1916): 460.

26
Land and Loan Office, perspectival rendering by Parker N. Berry. Reprinted from *Architectural Record* 39 (May 1916): 461.

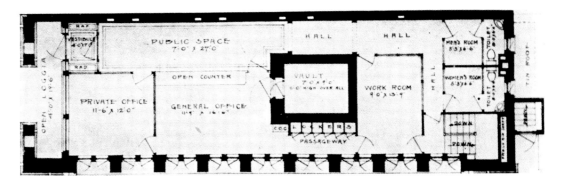

28
Land and Loan Office, plan of main floor.
Reprinted from *Architectural Record* 39
(May 1916): 460.

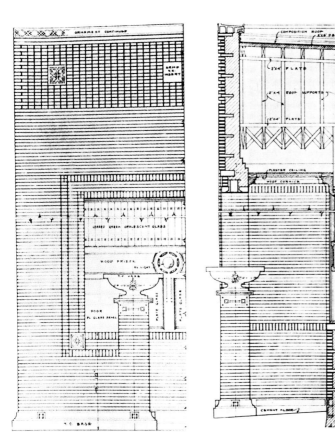

27a
Land and Loan Office, working drawing,
detail of front elevation. Reprinted from
***Architectural Record* 39 (May 1916): 462.**

27b
Land and Loan Office, working drawing,
detail of section through front elevation.
Reprinted from *Architectural Record* 39
(May 1916): 463.

ture of Democracy'' (1916) Rebori reviewed this work with two other banks: the Merchants National Bank in Grinnell, Iowa (1913–14) and the Home Building Association in Newark, Ohio (1914–15). He compared the Algona design with the others to show how Sullivan treated each building as a variation of unchanging principles determined by the related functions of these small town financial institutions. Rebori used the Algona Land and Loan Office to demonstrate that for Sullivan "no work [is] too small to receive or demand careful consideration and due study by a mature intellect."[14]

Although Sullivan was limited by material resources,[15] his design for the Algona building shows alternatives to the more pictorial and abstract solutions applied to the larger and costlier banks. While he reduced his means, he sustained their essential effects: polychromatic harmonies, modulated highlights and shadows, and the contrast of solids with voids and verticals with horizontals.

Here Sullivan used a limited range of chromatic materials to enhance and enliven the exterior surfaces (figures 27a, 27b). He contrasted the reddish hues of tinted pressed brick with high-gloss, glazed, green terra cotta insets: a relief cornice, a beveled base, and green and white terra cotta plaques in the capitals of the window piers. He applied the law of the simultaneous contrast of colors in the opalescent leaded glass windows, where he set gold cruciform patterns into mottled blue and violet fields. And since these windows are framed by brick, the colors of each surface intensify each other. Sullivan joined these color arrangements with patterns of textured brickwork to form a three-part division of base, wall, and cornice. With this three-part composition, he endowed the diminutive, self-contained block with a simple monumental presence.

The rectangular block also gains in monumentality through contrasting patterns of solids and voids and of highlights and shadows. For example, the side elevations are penetrated by deep-set rectangular windows that alternate with massive brick piers flush with the wall surface. While these piers are repeated on the main facade to frame the entrance, the vertical accents of the windows reinforce and balance the horizontal features of the entrance portico.[16]

Today only the rectangular volume and opalescent windows remain of the original interior layout and decoration. A floor plan, published in Rebori's 1916 review, illustrates how Sullivan reconceived the democratic plan under the most severe financial restrictions (figure 28). Although he placed the entrance to the left of the portico opening and the main axis, he aligned the entrance from the vestibule with an open public space. He then extended this longitudinal axis and horizontal vista through two adjoining halls that lead to the men's and women's rooms in the rear of the building. While placing the vault on the central axis, Sullivan framed this centerpiece with an open office space and a workroom. Such an arrangement saved the two most prominent features of his democratic plan: the visible accessibility of the open vault and the diffused chromatic light that permeates both public and private spaces. These two features remain constants in Sullivan's program for democratizing and naturalizing architecture; he continued to use them to dissolve the boundaries between utility and art.

Notes

1.
Sprague, ''Sullivan and his Chief Draftsmen,'' p. 433. In this catalogue entry, Sprague also dates the preliminary design ''about March 1913.''

2.
On 14 May 1913, the *Algona Upper Des Moines-Republican* (Vol. 11) reported under ''Local News'': ''Mr. and Mrs. H. C. Adams left for Chicago last Thursday evening where Mr. Adams will consult with the architect for his new building and arrange for the material to be used in its construction. He expects to start the building during the latter part of the month.''

3.
On 17 September 1913, the *Algona Upper Des Moines-Republican* reported: ''The new building for H. C. Adams is nearing completion. It is as substantial as well as one of the most handsome buildings in the state and will make convenient offices for Mr. Adams and his increasing business.'' No further notices about the building appeared in this local newspaper.

4.
For Sullivan's 1920 drawing of a terra cotta capital for this addition, see Sprague, *The Drawings of Louis Sullivan*, figure 61.

5.
See letter from F. H. Shaver, vice-president of Peoples Savings Bank (Cedar Rapids) to D. Van Allen, a Clinton, Iowa, businessman for whom Sullivan built a commercial building in 1913–15.

6.
This confusion may stem from the fact that Adams was also a vice-president of the Algona State Bank, which was being remod-

eled concurrently with the construction of Adams's own new building. The dates of the Algona State Bank remodeling are 2 April–29 October 1913. Local newspaper accounts never mention that Adams's building was to be a bank; it was always referred to as Adams's land and loan office. At the same time, reports include mention of Henry C. Adams's old and new office quarters in the Algona State Bank building; but these reports are connected with his position as bank vice-president. See *Algona Upper Des Moines-Republican* 11 (2 April 1913; 14 May 1913; 28 May 1913; 3 September 1913; 17 September 1913; 29 October 1913).

Morrison was the first to give the following account, which has persisted in written histories of Sullivan's building: ''Intended by Mr. Adams for a bank building, and designed by Sullivan as such, the contemplated bank failed to receive a charter and the building was first used as a real estate building known as the Land & Loan Office'' (*Louis Sullivan*, p. 217). Morrison may have assumed that this was to be a bank building since it includes many of the features common to the banks—and for this reason it is also here treated as a variation of the rural bank building type. Parker N. Berry assisted Sullivan with this design. Parker's wife some forty years later rehearsed this account when she recalled that the building was supposed to be for the Iowa State Bank, but that Adams never received a charter for the bank; see Hoffmann, ''Parker N. Berry,'' 9.

7.
In 1917 Berry worked on drawings for a second-story addition. Adams commissioned Sullivan to make other changes in 1920, for which he made sketches for terra cotta ornament. In 1921 the Druggists'

Mutual Insurance Company of Iowa purchased the building, adding on to it in 1951. The building is now known as the Henry C. Adams Building. See Hoffmann, ''Parker N. Berry,'' 9.

8.
Ibid., 9. Hoffmann also mentions Berry's widow, who attributed the entire design to Berry's hand. But John Zukowsky and Pauline Saliga, who also attribute the working drawings to Berry, based their conclusions on studying actual drawings, thereby avoiding Mrs. Berry's later account; see *Chicago Architects Design*, p. 71.

9.
Hoffmann, ''Parker N. Berry,'' 9.

10.
See illustrations of the First State Bank of Manlius in Hoffmann's article; and of the project for Lincoln State Bank in Zukowsky's and Saliga's *Chicago Architects Design*, p. 71.

11.
For examples of Prairie School bank designs similar to Berry's, see Severen's comparison of the Algona design with Frank Lloyd Wright's City National Bank of Mason City, Iowa (1909–10) in ''Sullivan and Wright,'' 16–17; and Elmslie and Purcell's Madison [Minnesota] State Bank (1913), in *The Prairie School Tradition*, p. 133.

12.
Sullivan, *Kindergarten Chats* (1918), p. 124; cf. ''To the Young Man in Architecture'' (1900); rpt. *Kindergarten Chats* (1918), p. 216.

13.
Morrison, *Louis Sullivan*, p. 217.

14.
Rebori, ''An Architecture of Democracy,'' 460.

15.
Pressed bricks and tiles were manufactured by the Algona Brick and Tile Works. This local firm had acquired a new pressed brick machine just as construction began for the Algona Land and Loan Office (for which 100,000 bricks were used). See company's advertisement in *Algona Upper Des Moines-Republican* 11 (14 May 1913).

Here, apparently, Sullivan lacked the direct control over craftsmanship that he maintained in the higher-budget projects; especially in working with Kristian Schneider and the American Terra Cotta Company. The brickwork lacks the refinements seen in the other banks. The terra cotta tiles and reliefs, fired with high-gloss glazes, lack the delicate carving and subtle nuances achieved with the mottled, salt-fired matte glazes used in the more costly bank structures. Similar observations can be made about the Purdue State Bank in West Lafayette, Indiana.

16.
This bank demonstrates that rough-cut pressed tinted brick arranged in abstract patterns can fulfill Schuyler's aesthetic demand for finish. By modulating the fascia under the cornice with checkered light and dark contrasts in courses of receding and projecting bricks, Sullivan—or Berry—avoided the austere starkness of contours and massing that characterize the earlier Cedar Rapids bank.

Reserve Square, intersection of State, South, and Vine Streets

West Lafayette, Indiana

Dates

Plans approved: 28 January 1914

Opening: 1 January 1915[1]

Cost

$14,600

Of all the banks, the Purdue State Bank has suffered most from aggressive remodeling and modernization (figure 29). A scarcity of visual and written documents prohibits a thorough investigation of the bank's original appearance and conditions of commission.[2] Neither floor plans nor vintage photographs have survived. We do know that the Purdue State Bank was chartered in 1910 and that Sullivan's design was for the bank's first building.[3] Once construction began, the building took about nine months to complete. Also apparent from the minimal cost and modest scale is that, as in the Algona commission, Sullivan had to adjust his formula to a severely limited budget.

We can assume that the Purdue State Bank directors hired Sullivan to advance their image as progressive midwestern bankers. By 1914 Sullivan had established his reputation as a master of the small town rural bank. Those bankers who did not make the "pilgrimage" to the National Farmers' Bank in Owatonna could learn of the practical solutions and the social meanings of Sullivan's democratic plan in a 1912 issue of *The Bankers Magazine,* which presented the Cedar Rapids bank with photographs and excerpts from Sullivan's own descriptions. Such widespread interest in his first two monumental banks certainly would have brought Sullivan to the attention of the West Lafayette bankers.

As in the case of the Algona Land and Loan Office, it seems that Sullivan realized he could not produce a complete work of art. Given the low building budget, he probably oversaw Parker N. Berry's more direct role in carrying out preliminary designs. By contrast, Sullivan began in the same year a more intensive involvement with the construction of the Merchants National Bank in Grinnell, Iowa, where he was free to realize a lavish decorative scheme. Nonetheless, in the West Lafayette bank Sulli-

van showed how to retain his standard solutions for the small town bank with minimal material means. As in the Algona composition, Berry left his personal mark with the more classicizing elements of the design.

For the Purdue State Bank, Sullivan varied the rectangular bank block to fit an unusual building site. The bank is located on a triangular lot, at the intersection where State Street, the main commercial thoroughfare, branches into two diagonal streets forming a Y-shape. At this site the building is the focal point of Reserve Square, the town's commercial center. Given this prestigious location, Sullivan reshaped the standard rectangle into a trapezoid, with the shortest side as the main entrance. When one approaches the building from State Street, the orthogonals of the mass seem to spread outward so as to increase the building's dimensions. The entrance, framed in green terra cotta relief, contrasts with the reddish-brown pressed brick elevations and provides a prominent terminus for the State Street axis. Its broadly overhanging straight pediment and projecting door jambs strengthen these effects. Yet this combination of architectural elements is a classical one, reminiscent of Berry's hand in the Algona design (figure 26). The square window piers of the side elevations are squat, which is also more consistent with Berry's system of proportions than with Sullivan's more attenuated forms.

As in the Algona building, Sullivan reduced the chromatic spectrum of the West Lafayette bank elevations to contrasting relationships of reddish brick tones (ranging from yellow through brown) and mottled green terra cotta reliefs. In these reliefs the high-gloss glazes span from green through yellow hues. Reliefs cast with Sullivan's organic ornament appear in the front entrance enframement and in the side window enframements. Smaller variations of these motifs form a narrow cornice band.

Additionally, yellow and white terra cotta relief plaques, inserted in the capitals of the window piers, combine with the green terra cotta reliefs to enhance the chromatic contrast of ornament with the brick walls. Finally, the obdurate brick mass is relieved with sculptural and textural modulations of patterned brickwork and rough-cut pressed brick.[4]

On the interior, Sullivan located the vault at the rear of the bank and on axis with the entrance. This arrangement is the only extant feature of Sullivan's democratic plan. A photograph from the 1950s indicates that without stained glass, the democratic plan does not wholly succeed (figure 29).[5] When plain plate glass was used for windows designed to emit diffused chromatic light into the open interior space, direct sunlight seems to have been too strong. This photograph shows window awnings on the side elevations, an expedient but not aesthetic way to reduce the intensity of natural light.

Notes

1.

Dates and costs from *The Lafayette Daily Courier* of 29 January 1914; 29 December 1914; and 1 January 1915. The first of these issues also reported that construction would begin in the spring. Sprague dates design for the building as "about December 1913" and for the ornament "about March 1914." He further documents fee payments to Sullivan on 20 January 1914 and 16 January 1916. See Sprague, "Sullivan and his Chief Draftsmen," p. 434.

2.

This structure is now a branch bank of the First National Bank, the result of a merger with the Purdue State Bank in 1957. At the bank and at the Tippecanoe Historical Society there are photographs of the building site before and immediately after the bank was built. A brief description of the bank appears in David Parrish's *Historic Architecture of Lafayette, Indiana* (West Lafayette, Indiana, 1978), p. 48. Unlike most local newspaper accounts of Sullivan's banks in other towns, brevity is typical of reports in *The Lafayette Daily Courier.* No longer than one paragraph, such reports did not even name Sullivan as the architect.

3.

According to the staff at the Tippecanoe Historical Society, the bank first occupied space in the row of commercial buildings on the north side of State Street. That premise was taken over by the clothier Henry Rosenthal after the bank moved (*The Lafayette Daily Courier,* 25 December 1914).

4.

Other qualities, similar to those in the Algona building, suggest Sullivan's peripheral involvement with the completion of his design. The high-gloss mottled green terra cotta relief, the terra cotta plaques above the window piers, and the surface brickwork lack the precision of finish and chromatic nuances characteristic of Sullivan's work when more funds were available.

5.

A contemporary view of the bank is published in the June 1924 issue of *Western Architecture,* an issue commemorating Sullivan following his death on 14 April 1924 (vol. 23, plate 23). The poor tonal contrast in this photographic reproduction has made it impossible to reproduce here.

N.W. corner Fourth and Broad Streets

Grinnell, Iowa

Dates

Preliminary sketches: 28 November 1913 (plan); 30 November 1913 (elevations)

Working drawings: 30 January, 28 February 1914

Official opening: 1 January 1915

National Historic Landmark: 1976

Addition: 1975

Dimensions

42 × 75 × 35 feet

Cost

$60,000

Sullivan designed the Merchants National Bank[1] simultaneously with the Land and Loan Office and the Purdue State Bank. Whereas these two designs are studies in restrained simplicity, the Merchants National Bank is a study in restrained luxury. This work earned for itself, and for several of Sullivan's other banks, the popular rubric of "jewel box." For the Grinnell bank, much smaller than its counterpart in Owatonna, Sullivan compressed his polychromatic materials into a reduced scale and greatly enhanced their glowing, jewel-like qualities (plate 5).

At both Owatonna and Grinnell, the clients sought out Sullivan for his artistic as much as his practical skills. The directors of the Grinnell bank, planning "a new and modern bank," had visited the Owatonna bank in mid-November 1913. Almost immediately upon their return they invited Sullivan to begin their building project. By 28 November 1913 Sullivan was in Grinnell making preliminary drawings for the elevations and layout.[2]

Extensive narrative and visual documents recording Sullivan's design process during his initial visit make this bank historically important. A. N. Rebori's 1916 review of the Grinnell bank records details of this event and illustrates the preliminary on-site sketches, drawn on stationery from the drugstore next to the bank site (figures 1–3). Later, Sullivan made the sketches available to Rebori during a personal interview. Through Rebori's narrative we can gain access to Sullivan's organic design methods for solving artistic and practical problems quickly and in accordance with his client's needs. He first noted the physical acts involved in Sullivan's creative process:

For three whole days he talked, drew, rubbing out as changes were made, fitting and adjusting to the satisfaction of all. . . . I asked Mr. Sullivan how it happened that his preliminary sketches were worked out in such definite manner, and he answered quite simply that "those were the requirements as given, and it only remained to jot them down on paper," which he did, using sheets ["of common yellow paper acquired at a near-by apothecary shop"] available at the time.

Rebori also reported Sullivan's dialogue with his clients. He wrote that since Sullivan worked on these sketches "in a little office adjoining the president's room in the old bank building in view of and with the aid of the building committee . . . the owner knew exactly what the finished building would look like before Sullivan left."[3]

Rebori's discussion of Sullivan's creative process also indicates how Sullivan arrived at spontaneous, intuitively conceived, yet rational solutions to practical problems. Rebori used Sullivan's own evolutionary theories of the creative process to explain the organic continuum of initial sketches, functional plan, and the finished building:

The development of the sketches into working drawings proceeded in close accordance with the original scheme, for, having once determined the exact conditions and requirements, there was no further need for change, for the *vital organ,* the plan, which plays the important role, was determined upon and accepted. Hence we see how Sullivan arrives in a most intimate manner to a logical expression of the functioning duties of the building itself [emphasis added].[4]

We can share Rebori's admiration: Sullivan's finished building corresponds very closely to these first notations, which can be studied in the extant original drawings, now in the Bentley Historical Collection, University of Michigan.

Rebori's account shows that throughout his career Sullivan continued to apply the methods of composition he had learned at the Ecole des Beaux-Arts, where he was a student in 1874–75. There he was taught to render the *esquisse,* that is, the spontaneous notations of the layout and their resulting elevations, shaped by practical solutions to the building program. The artistic merit of these first sketches was then judged by the degree to which the original solutions were sustained throughout the design process, ending with the final scheme. These lessons were repeated at every stage of the student's education, conditioning him to practice this method during his entire career. Sullivan rethought this academic procedure in organic terms so as to supplant mechanical with natural processes as the model for artistic creation. In his theoretical writings, he replaced the academic term, "composition," with "organization," a word he adapted from biological discourse.[5]

Contemporary critics, who saw the Merchants National Bank firsthand, help us appreciate its compositional integrity.[6] For example, in a 1916 issue of the *Western Architect,* a reviewer admired the way that Sullivan harmonized mass with proportion, ornament, and color, making this bank "one of Sullivan's best commercial buildings."[7] In fact, Sullivan's preliminary sketch for the main elevation shows that he used primary geometric forms and simple arithmetic proportions to integrate visually the solids and voids and the ornamental enframements of the parts with the whole. This observation, together with Rebori's account of Sullivan's actual location when he drew the preliminary designs, offer starting points for assessing the formal and chromatic composition as Sullivan's studied artistic response to the external and internal conditions of the building program.

A vintage photograph shows the Merchants National Bank with the adjacent commercial buildings (figure 5). This document invites a reassessment of the bank design since previously published photographs have isolated the bank from its original setting, prompting later viewers to question the integrity of Sullivan's design.[8] The earlier photograph now reclaims for the Grinnell bank what the anonymous *Architectural Record* critic praised in the Owatonna bank—Sullivan's dual success in weaving the building into the existing town fabric and in asserting its self-referentiality.

Sullivan was required to design the new Grinnell bank on the site of the old bank building—at the major intersection of turn-of-the-century Grinnell.[9] This intersection separates the commercial and civic districts. While working in the old structure, Sullivan surely realized that such a location demanded a visual and conceptual transition between two kinds of community activities and their building types. Sullivan responded to these contextual problems in two ways: by deriving abstract formal patterns from the commercial facades and textures, colors, and massing from the nearby civic monuments.

In designing the elevations, Sullivan combined and, thereby continued, the dimensions, rhythms, and patterns of the commercial buildings that line both sides of Fourth Street and the west side of Broad Street. On the Broad Street elevation, he made the attenuated colonnettes of the window, recessed within the wall, echo the vertical rhythms of the pier and lintel fenestration in the adjacent buildings. For the main Fourth Street elevation, Sullivan abstracted circles and squares from the segmented- and flat-arch second-story window pediments on the buildings lining the block. Sullivan enlarged and overlapped these geometric forms and combined them with botanical motifs (figure 30). This combination became the rose window medallion above the bank's entrance.[10]

Sullivan also made the bank interact with the more overt revival style buildings that occupy the opposite corners of the intersection at Fourth and Broad streets. He composed a reddish brick rectangular block and adorned it with gilded and buff-brown ornamental reliefs to match the proportions, textures, and polychromy of the Richardsonian Romanesque public library to the east. In a similar way, Sullivan restated the red brick and rusticated sandstone elevations of the four-storied, turreted Romanesque revival commercial building to the south.

Sullivan distinguished the Merchants National Bank from the neighboring buildings by making a self-contained image of modern commercial and building conditions; he made the salient features of the exterior refer to the functional layout and the decorative program of the interior. He varied the scale and dimensions of the windows according to the interior spaces they illuminate (figures 31, 32). He designated the two-story height of the public banking hall with both the rose window over the main entrance and the elevated horizontal range of side windows. Similarly, he inserted smaller, but more precisely cut, rectangular windows into the ground story or "base." These windows more directly illuminate the director's office and women's room, areas partitioned off from the main banking space and indirectly lit by the skylight and clerestory windows (figures 33, 34).

The rose window medallion is a leitmotif that conveys the social functions of the bank and that gives artistic unity to the whole. Recently, one historian has identified the relief pattern as a "key" that symbolizes the radiating metal spokes of the locks on the vault doors.[11] This is a judicious but somewhat limited observation. We might extend this "key" metaphor to consider the ways the medallion refers to the interior layout and decorative scheme and, in turn, to Sullivan's ritualization of the banking activity.

30
**Merchants National Bank, Grinnell, Iowa,
1913–15. Detail of entrance. Photo: Henry
Fuermann, Chicago Architectural Photographing Co.**

31
Merchants National Bank, main floor plan
and longitudinal section looking west.
Reprinted from *Western Architect* 23
(February 1916).

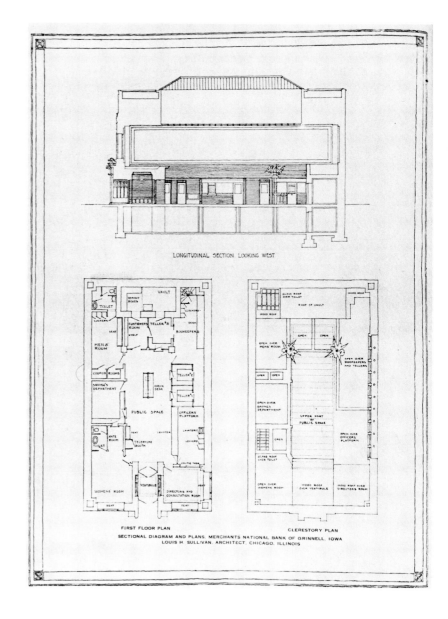

32
Merchants National Bank, view of public space toward vault. Photo: Henry Fuermann, Chicago Architectural Photographing Co.

33
Merchants National Bank, director's and consultation room. Reprinted from *Western Architect* 23 (February 1916).

34
Merchants National Bank, women's room. Photo: Henry Fuermann, Chicago Architectural Photographing Co.

For example, Sullivan used the square, circle, and botanical forms to show how the mechanical is continuous with the organic. Such a synthesis between geometry and natural forms is the essence of his objective-subjective symbolism for ornament and architecture. Sullivan considered this vital interaction between the mechanistic-objective and the organic-subjective to be the metaphysical basis for achieving insights of a transcendental democracy. (That is, Sullivan believed that by actually seeing these symbolic forms the spectator would be free to realize his or her identity with the Infinite Creative Spirit and, then, contribute to the moral, physical, and spiritual advance of society at large.) In the Grinnell bank Sullivan extended the objective-subjective continuum from his ornament and surface planes into architectural layout. At either end of the major axis, he aligned the exterior organic image of the rose window medallion with the interior mechanical image of the vault. On the interior, he reinforced this visual and conceptual analogy by placing the desk and water fountain along the same central axis.

Extensive alterations to the interior of the Grinnell bank have eradicated important features of Sullivan's holistic design.[12] But the earliest critics noted the reciprocity between the interior and exterior. According to Rebori:

If the exterior frankly proclaims the plan, it is to the interior that we must turn to see the plan in working order. . . . The direct and simple treatment of the front, depending largely on its color scheme for interest, truthfully corresponds to the interior forms or plan.

Rebori also observed how the mechanized vault became the focal point of the organic, democratic plan:

From the moment the visitor enters past the vestibuled doors the workings of the bank are thrown open to view, disclosing at first sight the intricate mechanism of the open doors to the steel-lined vaults on the central axis. Then comes to view on the right and left of the glass, brick and bronze partition screens that divide the space around the central public lobby. It is like the open works of a watch as seen through its crystal back cover.[13]

Sullivan composed other elements of reciprocity by making the pattern of the rose window medallion the dominant theme for the exterior and interior reliefs (figure 30). Thus, throughout the whole design, he reused the concave, hexagonal, shield-like form that results from overlapping circles and squares. This polygonal shape reappears on the exterior in the band of relief forming the cornice. In the interior, the shield form appears in the reliefs above the vault, in the architrave over the partition that screens the vault, in the leaded glass patterns of the rose window, and in the mosaic pattern of the clock over the vestibule (figures 32, 35; plates 6, 7).

Sullivan also used polychromy to establish the reciprocity between interior and exterior and between the parts and the whole. Originally, the brick elevations were richly colored with shades of blue-black to golden-red.[14] Sullivan continued the dominantly reddish-brown hue of the elevations in the terra cotta relief cornice. But for the rose window medallion he used a predominantly buff-toned glaze, adding green to receding planes and gilding high-relief surfaces. This combination enlivens the medallion relief and, by way of complementary color contrast, adds to the chromatic richness of the whole. Sullivan further guaranteed a uniform radiance for the exterior with gilded three-dimensional motifs. On the side elevation he gilded the window colonnettes, matching the brilliance of the gilt winged lions that frame the main entrance. Furthermore, Sullivan used the exterior chromatic composition to introduce the spectator/user to the golden illumination of the interior.

35
Merchants National Bank, diagonal view toward director's and consultation room and vestibule. Photo: Henry Fuermann, Chicago Architectural Photographing Co.

36
Merchants National Bank, men's room.
Photo: Henry Fuermann, Chicago Archi-
tectural Photographing Co.

37
Merchants National Bank, view of en-
trance into tellers' and bookkeepers'
spaces. Reprinted from *Western Architect*
23 (February 1916).

38
Merchants National Bank, detail of check
desk in public space. Photo: Henry Fuer-
mann, Chicago Architectural Photograph-
ing Co.

Inside the building, gilded reliefs originally combined with diffused chromatic light to evoke "abundant warm daylight."[15] Sullivan created such an ambience by mixing natural light filtered through the contrasting color compositions of the rose window and the clerestory window. In the rose window, radial and spiral patterns of highly saturated red, orange, and yellow hues dominate the complementary color patterns of cooler greens and blues (plate 7). Sullivan reversed this chromatic relationship in the clerestory windows (figures 35, 38), where geometric patterns are rendered in blues and greens against contrasting hues of mottled purple and yellow. Sullivan also reproduced natural golden light by surrounding the opalescent blue skylight over the banking hall with closely spaced, tiny incandescent light bulbs (figure 36).

Sullivan mixed all these reflecting, filtered chromatic lights to enliven and dematerialize the unadorned plastered surfaces of the west clerestory wall. He may have done so to overcome the restrictions of a building budget that prohibited mural painting. In any case, the reflected light from colored glass (in the lamps and electroliers, as well as the east window and skylight) produced "a mottled soft colored flat tone of vibrating transparency" on the clerestory wall.[16] Here Sullivan used the bare wall as a picture plane, capturing the free play of transient light. In this way he rendered again the themes of nature depicted with figurative imagery and fresco patterns in the interiors of the Owatonna and Cedar Rapids banks.

For the subordinate color scheme, Sullivan used natural materials that enhance the ambience of golden tones: verde antique marble counter tops; hickory stained wood; speckled buff salt-glazed Roman brick veneers; and pinkish-gray Tennessee marble floors. He composed these natural materials and the surfaces they adorn to enhance another kind of artistic unity. He maintained a structural, rectilinear unity throughout this scintillating interior with architectonic woodwork, Craftsman-style furniture and cabinetwork, and square brick piers surmounted by square-topped decorative urns (figures 32, 36–38).

When the Merchants National Bank was completed, a local newspaper recalled that while the bank was undergoing construction, its novel appearance had incited negative reactions among the townspeople. But when the bank opened, the public responded enthusiastically by praising its practical, technological, and artistic innovations. They considered the practical features, such as the easy access to public telephones and restrooms, indicative of the bank's role as a public servant. They admired Sullivan's ventilation system (which continuously circulated fresh air) as a sign of modern technological innovation.

Local viewers were most impressed by Sullivan's artistic innovations—the chromatic brilliance of the whole and the warm illumination of the interior—which inspired speculations about his artistic genius and his source of creative inspiration. For example, one writer claimed:

The new Merchants Bank building is not a mere building. It is a creation. It was realized first in the mind of Louis H. Sullivan. Mr. Sullivan dreamed the building. The building is his dream come true.[17]

Yet another writer attempted to describe the exotic content of the ''dream'':

The man who drew the designs must have steeped himself in the atmosphere of the Arabian Nights, Arabian Days and the Tales of Persian Fireworshippers until it worked like hasheesh and the subconscious mind took control and saw, in a vision, the complete semblance of the thing that was to be. . . . Shutting himself up almost without food, he concentrates every thought upon his work as zealously as a Buddhist priest sinks his identity in the larger thought of Nirvana.[18]

These journalists may have met Sullivan during one of his visits to Grinnell and heard him explain his metaphysical sources of inspiration, a theoretical explanation that invites dream-like interpretations. But these laymen missed another, equally important, part of Sullivan's architectural theory. Sullivan designed the Grinnell bank within its setting to illustrate his idea that a modern, American architecture must be rooted in earlier historical styles. As the vintage photograph of this bank makes clear, however, Sullivan did not simply imitate the outward forms of these styles. Rather, he demonstrated that a new style results only when the architect joins modern artistic materials, building techniques, and social programs with the abstract, universal principles of design embodied in historical stylistic forms.

Sullivan realized that his commissions for small town banks depended more on his technological and practical expertise than on his messianic artistic mission. Two years after the completion of the Grinnell bank, he used the photographic postcard of the bank to announce his professional skills (figure 5). In 1917 he presented it to the directors of the Peoples Savings Bank in Sidney, Ohio, with an inscription outlining the bank's vital statistics: the dimensions, the cost, and the signature of the architect.

Notes

1.
Now occupied by Poweshiek County Bank.

2.
See Severens, "Louis Sullivan Builds a Small-Town Bank," 68. Severens provides a thorough documentation of the conditions of the commission, noting that Bennett had the calling card of the president of the Grinnell bank, George Hamlin, and that Bennett sent it to Purcell and Elmslie, hoping to get the Grinnell bank commission for them. See also announcement of bank's plans to build new building in *The Grinnell Herald* 45 (11 September 1913): 1.

3.
Rebori, "An Architecture of Democracy," 438.

4.
Ibid., 441; cf. Sullivan, "The Tall Office Building Artistically Considered."

5.
See, for example, Sullivan, *Kindergarten Chats* (1901), p. 231. Cf. Sullivan's statements regarding the valuable lessons derived from the academic logical design process in "Sullivan's answer to Elmer Grey [a report from the second annual convention of the Architectural League of America]," in *Brickbuilder* 9 (June 1900): 113; 25 July 1904 letter from Sullivan to Claude Bragdon on microfilm at the Burnham Library of the Art Institute of Chicago. For a discussion of the *esquisse* method and Sullivan's renderings for ornament, see Sprague, *The Drawings of Louis Sullivan*, p. 11.

6.
Later critics and historians approved of Sullivan's organic design process. They considered it progressive, contributing to a modern "functionalist" style. However, they often chastised Sullivan for his use of ornament (see note 38 in the historical survey above). The modernist critical view of Sullivan's designs for the exterior elevations of the Grinnell bank typify some of the problems in assessing Sullivan's banks through black-and-white photographs. In these elevations, Sullivan emphasized the juxtaposition between large-scale and bold ornamental relief and the simple rectangular mass. Black-and-white photographs exaggerate such contrasts. Modernist viewers perceived these juxtapositions, and what seemed to be unrelated elevations, as dissonant formal relationships. As a result, they regarded the Grinnell bank composition as a whole to be "a falling off in Sullivan's work." See, for example, Bush-Brown, *Louis Sullivan*, p. 31.

7.
"The Works of Sullivan an Inspiration rather than a Model," *Western Architect* 23 (February 1916): 20.

8.
See note 6 above.

9.
The bank directors required that the old bank clock be placed on the corner of the new building.

10.
Sprague has identified Parker N. Berry's hand in these decorative motifs; see "Louis Sullivan and his Chief Draftsmen," p. 157.

11.
Severens, "Louis Sullivan Builds a Small-Town Bank," 69.

12.
This original axial alignment was destroyed when the rear wall of the original structure was opened to a later addition. Sullivan's use of the continuous grille, glass, and brick pier partition in front of the vault and tellers' cages may have been determined by his clients. While this arrangement detracts from the more direct axial vista he first introduced in the Cedar Rapids bank interior, Sullivan still attained the openness and clear visibility of the parts within the whole. He adapted the same materials and structural elements of the earlier bank to this modified version of the democratic plan—polished plate glass partitions, interrupted only by structural piers that also mark subordinate banking spaces, and unadorned vertical bronze grilles for the tellers' cages.

13.
Rebori, "An Architecture of Democracy," 441, 449. One reviewer expected to see mural paintings on the clerestory walls: "The interior is detailed in brick and tile and finished above in panels suggestive of mural subjects, particularly at the end of the banking room" ("Works of Sullivan an Inspiration," 20).

14.
Rebori, "An Architecture of Democracy," 449.

15.
"The Merchant National's Fine Building," *The Grinnell Herald* 47 (5 January 1915), n.p.

16.
Rebori, "An Architecture of Democracy," 449, 453.

17.
"The Merchant National's Fine Building."

18.
Cited in Severens, "Louis Sullivan Designs a Small-Town Bank," 71.

N.W. corner Main and North Third Streets

Newark, Ohio

Dates

Commission received: 30 March 1914[1]

Working drawings: 8 August 1914[2]

Official opening: 24 August 1915

Dimensions

60 × 22 feet

Cost

$39,000

When the Home Building Association commissioned Sullivan to design a new building, it was one of the largest financial institutions in Newark.[3] This savings and loan company was proud that it served only local townspeople and real estate development and that its own growth benefited the town's expansion. Upon completion of their new quarters, the owners boasted that they had outgrown their old building, making "the new home . . . imperative," and that "this [new] building is evidence of what thrift and savings have already accomplished."[4] Located on one of the most prominent sites in Newark, the new building, with its "beauty, durability, and progressiveness in architectural design,"[5] signaled the bank's own progressive, stable, and prominent position in the community.

The town of Newark is laid out on a gridiron plan with the Licking County Courthouse and Newark Square at its center. The Home Building Association structure is located on a small corner lot at the intersection of the main east-west coordinate of the grid and faces the four-story courthouse building. Two conditions—the need for spacious quarters on a small lot and the immediate presence of a civic monument—determined Sullivan's final scheme, which differs from the other banks. Here Sullivan designed a two-story brick structure above a finished basement and covered it in greyish-green terra cotta (figures 39, 40). His choice of facing materials and his treatment of ornament in the Newark bank can be explained primarily by the bank's setting,[6] but the use of terra cotta rather than tinted pressed brick also demonstrates how he varied the textures and hues of standardized building materials for a standardized building type. When he had performed this exercise in his skyscrapers, Sullivan explained that such artistic variations were a way to individualize buildings within a generic type.[7]

Sullivan designed each elevation of the new bank building to be continuous with the commercial buildings facing Newark Square and, at the same time, to be part of an enframement for the Second Empire style courthouse. The courthouse asserts its civic and judicial authority with the grandiose proportions and high-relief embellishments typical of nineteenth-century county courthouses throughout the northeastern United States.[8] Each of the elevations and the central tower of the building are adorned with classical motifs and figurative sculpture. These embellishments, carved in buff-colored sandstone, project boldly from greenish-gray limestone surfaces. As variations of the ornate Second Empire style, the surrounding commercial buildings are faced with common red brick and detailed with strongly modeled Italianate motifs and bracketed cornices.

In Newark, Sullivan's problem was to design a small-scale structure that would hold its own in relation to these buildings. He solved this problem with the abstract elements of design: contour, color, texture, and proportion. Sullivan rendered the right angles of the gridiron in three dimensions and made the classical modules and massing of neighboring commercial facades more geometrically abstract. In so doing he provided an ordered closure for their irregular elevations. The proportions of the Newark bank conform with those of the existing commercial buildings, but the colors and textures of the mass do not. This bank consequently lacks the subtle integration with similar building types that Sullivan developed in the other banks. Instead, it carries on a more direct dialogue with the monumental civic centerpiece.

The Newark bank design can be appreciated best in its relation to the courthouse. Sullivan used abstract geometric patterns to make the building a self-contained unit, but he also combined these patterns with organic motifs to represent the system of rectilineation underlying the classical motifs of the courthouse elevations. Rebori's firsthand descriptions, and Sullivan's own remarks, bring to our attention the compositional harmony of the original bank elevations. Rebori admired Sullivan's "emphasis and subordination . . . in the placement and scale of his decoration." He regarded Sullivan's boldly modeled reliefs among his best strategies for overcoming the building's diminutive size. Rebori also understood the analogic functions of ornament, as representing interior spatial and structural realities and functional hierarchies. He applied this analogy when he explained Sullivan's placement of "the delicate burst of floral ornament" on either side of the large rectangle that frames the two stories on the side elevation. He also quoted Sullivan's explanation that such an arrangement "[took] the eye away from the side [entrance] so that the front entrance would dominate and clearly mark the public entrance to the building."[9]

By developing a self-referential theme of rectilineation, Sullivan both unified and differentiated the side and the front elevations. He subdivided the larger framing rectangle of the side elevation into the horizontal window ranges of the ground and second stories. He placed a green mosaic panel, with the bank's name detailed in gold, between these two floors to define their functions and to reassert a horizontal direction to the rear and front entrances. At the same time, Sullivan designed the horizontal side elevations to continue the orthogonals of the courthouse.

On the front elevation Sullivan restated these rectilinear enframements in a vertical direction to make the main facade conform with the dimensions of the courthouse and the adjacent commercial buildings. Sullivan asserted the bank's commercial, civic presence by emphasizing the "tallness" of the two-story building. As in the skyscrapers, he reinforced the

39
Home Building Association, Newark,
Ohio, 1914–15. Photo: Henry Fuermann,
Chicago Architectural Photographing Co.

40
Home Building Association, east facade.
Photo: Henry Fuermann, Chicago Archi-
tectural Photographing Co.

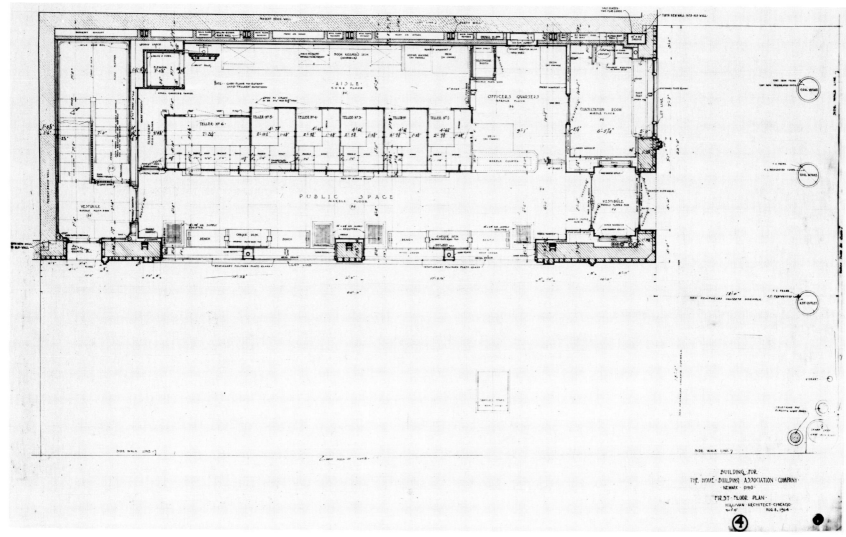

41
Home Building Association, working drawing of first floor plan. Photo: Henry Fuermann, Chicago Architectural Photographing Co.

42
Home Building Association, working drawing of second floor plan. Photograph of microfilm, The Art Institute of Chicago.

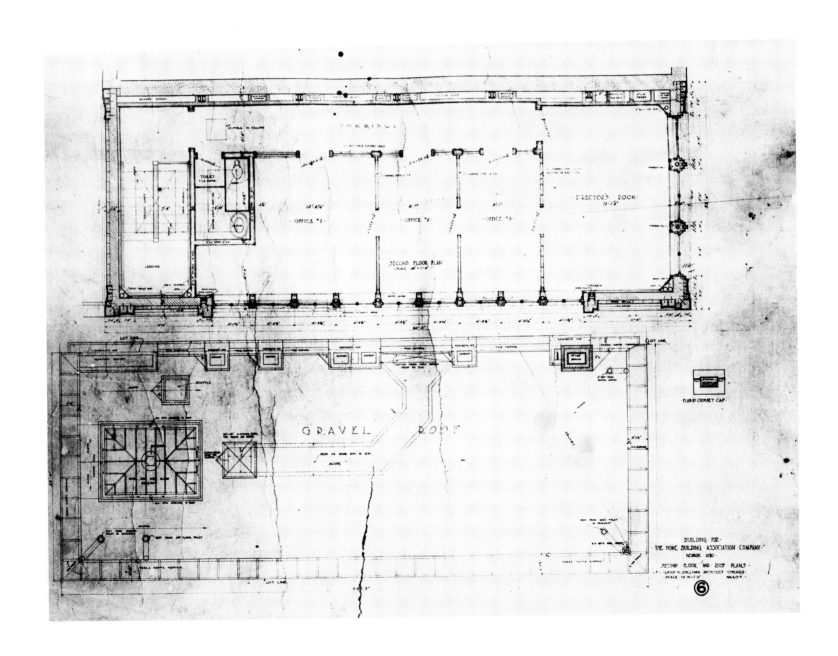

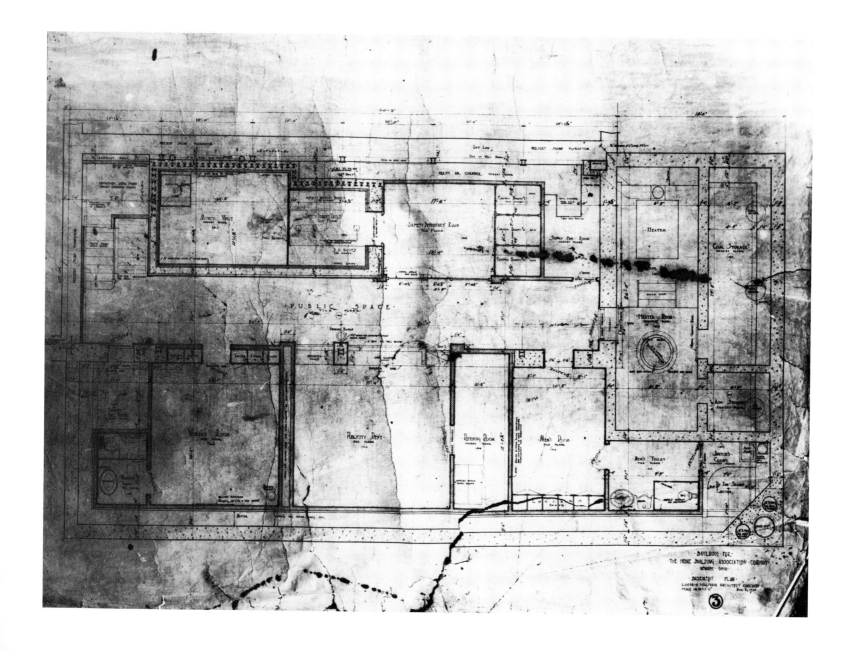

43
**Home Building Association, working
drawing of basement plan. Photograph of
microfilm, The Art Institute of Chicago.**

44
**Home Building Association, view toward
rear entrance. Photo: Henry Fuermann,
Chicago Architectural Photographing Co.**

45
Home Building Association, detail of light
troughs and ceiling frescoes. Photo:
Henry Fuermann, Chicago Architectural
Photographing Co.

vertical dimension with a slender colonnette surmounted with a flourish of ornament and placed in the center of the facade. This centerpiece also mediates and balances the contrasting vertical door and horizontal window. Finally, Sullivan renewed his collaboration with Millet to translate the scrolls, leaf forms, and tonal gradations of the terra cotta reliefs into brilliantly colored mosaic patterns. This network of organic and geometric motifs frames the association's former name, "The Old Home," within its triangular insignia (plate 8).

Sullivan's layout for the Newark bank indicates that he could vary the features of the democratic plan to suit the specific requirements of each new commission (figure 41). Since this structure was to function as a bank as well as an office building, Sullivan placed the main banking hall on the ground story and moved the director's and service offices to the second story (figure 42). He completed the practical functions of his plan in the basement (figure 43), where he located the publicity room, public women's and men's meeting and rest rooms, and the lower, main section of a two-story vault designed specifically for this space.[10]

Originally the spectator/user would have entered the main banking hall from a small vestibule located to the left of the central axis (figure 44). From this point, one would have had a direct, axial view of the public banking space. To the right of this space one gained a full view into the open officers' area and glass-partitioned tellers' cages. The upper portion of the two-story vault was located behind the tellers' cages in the northeast corner of the bank. To make this vault clearly visible despite its obscure location, Sullivan may have introduced here, for the first time, continuous glass partitions between the public and working spaces. He joined polished plate glass partitions with small bronze clamps instead of framing piers so that the glazed screens in front of the tellers' spaces

were virtually uninterrupted, except for bronze grille wickets. Such a revision of the democratic plan is a significant one, since it greatly enhanced the visual coherence and accessibility of the interior banking facilities.

Sullivan augmented this spatial openness with diffused natural and artificial light. He arranged continuous horizontal windows directly over the public banking space so that natural light penetrated into the tellers' area. He also placed continuous bronze light troughs over the tellers' work spaces (figure 45) and added lamps to the tellers' desks. As a result, all working areas had abundant illumination. Light permeated every space; it also reflected from every surface, whether polished plate glass, marble, or wood. When these direct, diffused, and reflected lights interacted with the chromatic effects of the natural facing materials and the stenciled frescoes, the spectator witnessed a dazzling architectural spectacle.[11]

Despite the diminutive size of the banking hall, it was lavishly treated with rich natural materials and color harmonies. Intricately veined, "rare antique" black marble covered the floor, continued over the counter tops, and lined the dadoes of the surrounding walls. Mahogany Craftsman-style furniture and carved ceiling beams complemented "doors of carefully selected grained African mahogany veneer from the Togas Islands off the coast of Africa."[12] Sullivan reiterated these dark brown natural hues in fresco patterns of intertwining shields, triangles, spirals, and botanical motifs rendered against a field of brick red and detailed in green, blue, and buff gold (plate 9).[13]

The dominant colors and motifs of the interior frescoes refer back to the exterior. The reddish-brick hue established a complementary contrast with the grayish-green exterior. (Here Sullivan reversed the chromatic relationships he had created in the banks designed with brick-faced exteriors and green-hued interiors.) He also repeated the color spectrum of the mosaic panel on the main facade in the interior stencil patterns.

When the bank owners commissioned Sullivan's design, they were joining a larger civic-reform campaign. Civic leaders sought to reverse a reputation for lawlessness that the town acquired under local prohibition laws. Responding to the patriotism of the City Beautiful movement, the Newark coalition embarked on a building program to enhance the townscape and attract new business to the area.[14] In fact, when the Home Building Association was completed, local journalists added it to a list of new architectural monuments that made Newark "a city of beautiful architecture."[15] The local press also recorded the original artistic and civic prominence Sullivan's design briefly enjoyed, calling it "Newark's most beautiful building of which every citizen is justly proud."[16] Unfortunately, this "jewel" has been neglected and defaced. The interior has been entirely gutted; the exterior has been marred by the enlargement of windows and the removal of the ground story corner pier.

Notes

1.
Reported in "Architect is selected for new [Home Loan Association] building" in *Newark Daily Advocate* 81 (30 March 1914): 5. Other reports include announcement of the demolition of old structure on building site (21 July 1914) and of costs and building permits issued (10 August 1914).

2.
A complete set of working drawings are on microfilm at the Burnham Library of The Art Institute of Chicago. These renderings were loaned to the Library by W. J. Camlin Company (General Contractors and Engineers, Newark, Ohio) on 17 April 1951 (letter from W. J. Camlin to John G. Replinger, Burnham Library).

3.
Originally named the Old Home Loan Association, the Home Building Association was founded in 1880 to serve as a savings and loan association for real estate; it did not serve commercial banking. See "New Building to be Built by 'Old Home,' " *Newark Daily Advocate* 81 (14 July 1914): 10. The association did not survive the effects of the 1929 crash, and with changing ownerships the building served a variety of functions. When Morrison published his monograph in 1935, the building was owned by the Union Trust Company. It has also been used as a jewelry store, a clothing store, and in 1984 as an ice cream parlor. Little information exists regarding the building history of the bank; the following discussion is taken from "Opening of New Quarters Home Building Ass'n," *Newark American Tribune* 89 (25 August 1915): 3.

4.
Bank advertisement, *Newark American Tribune* 68 (24 August 1915): 7. The Home Building Association was so successful that they required additional spaces for a publicity and advertising room as well as the more standard office space.

5.
"New Building to be Built by 'Old Home.' "

6.
Considering the built environment and the association's prestige, we might question Morrison's suggestion that Sullivan's use of greenish-gray terra cotta for the Newark Bank was simply an economic, and ill-considered, choice. Morrison wrote, "The general effect of the exterior is not good, and one has the feeling that the whole enterprise was cheap" (*Louis Sullivan*, p. 219).

7.
For example, Sullivan dressed the entire Guaranty Building with reddish-brown terra cotta reliefs, the superstructure of the Gage Building with white terra cotta, and the superstructure of the Schlesinger-Mayer Store with white glazed terra cotta tile. See also Sullivan's explanation of this function of ornament in "Ornament in Architecture," 189.

8.
See Richard Pare, *Court House: A Photographic Document* (New York: Horizon Press, 1978).

9.
Rebori, "An Architecture of Democracy," 450. As the plan shows, the vertical markers are also ventilation shafts.
   Sprague attributes the style of the relief ornament on the side elevation to Sulli-

van's draftsman at this time, Parker N. Berry; see "Louis Sullivan and his Chief Draftsmen," p. 157.

10.

The Home Building Association dedicated its women's room "to the Women of Newark . . . [hoping that] the women [would] take advantage of [it] and feel free to come there at all times." Both a side entry and the main entrance provided easy access to this facility. The bankers also took pride in the unique two-story vault. Apparently, Sullivan had to revise his plans to accommodate a vault that was too large for the main banking hall. The vault was extended, with a hydraulic elevator, into the basement, where the main vault was located; see "Opening of New Quarters," 3.

11.

Critical readings of vintage black-and-white photographs of the Newark bank interior illustrate how critics and historians have responded to Sullivan's works according to their own architectural values. In his 1916 article, Rebori cautioned the reader that the reflected light from the glass partitions and marble surfaces caused distortions in the photographs, making the interior look "flimsy." He argued that the whole was "harmoniously blended, rich and effective and well united and held in place." Rebori, like Sullivan, was more concerned with artistic refinements than with direct functionalist representation; Morrison exploited the photographic distortions to describe Sullivan's reductivist procedures and modernist achievements. Morrison considered the glass partitions the best part of the design, since the multiple reflections gave the functional arrangement of the interior "the gleaming precision of fine machinery." Although Morrison devalued the "lyrical en-

richments [of Sullivan's] ornament," his mechanistic analogy was to ensure Sullivan a place in the historical development of modernism. Cf. Rebori, "An Architecture of Democracy," 450, and Morrison, *Louis Sullivan*, p. 219.

12.

Rebori, "An Architecture of Democracy," 450.

13.

Morrison, *Louis Sullivan*, p. 219.

14.

See "Summary and Conclusions," *Industrial Survey of Licking County, Ohio* (unpublished ms. 1917), p. 4; and "Editorial: Neglected treasure located in Newark," *Advocate* (7 March 1979): 2.

15.

See "Newark is City of Beautiful Architecture," *Newark American Tribune* 68 (31 July 1915): 2. This article was written a month before the Home Building Association was completed and did not mention the new bank. However, in the announcement of the building project and the review of the opening of the bank, a strong connection was made between this earlier building activity and the construction of the new bank. In the former case, it was anticipated that the new bank building would "be an ornamental and welcome addition to the modern business houses of Newark" ("New Building to be Built by 'Old Home' ").

16.

See "Opening of New Quarters," 3.

S.E. corner Court Street and Ohio Avenue

Sidney, Ohio

Dates

Preliminary sketches: 15 December 1916

Call for bidders: 12 April 1917

Working drawings and specification sheets: 8 May–9 July 1917[1]

Official opening: 31 May 1918

National Historic Landmark Status: 1965

Dimensions

42 × 110 feet

Cost

$86,000, preliminary estimate

It is said that Sullivan considered the Peoples Savings and Loan Association his best bank design (figure 46).[2] Fortunately, it is also one of the best preserved of the banks, thanks to the local residents and bank directors who have sustained an awareness of the bank's artistic and historical significance. Today we can study this structure almost exactly as it was originally designed.[3]

As in the commissions for the banks in Owatonna and Grinnell, Sullivan's overall success in Sidney was due to an individual on the building committee who took a personal interest in the architect's work. LaFayette M. Studevant, the secretary of the bank, exemplified Sullivan's best bank clients. Like Owatonna's Carl Bennett, Studevant combined his entrepreneurial acumen, artistic awareness, and sense of civic responsibility to enable Sullivan to design for the bank a complete work of art.

Studevant had heard of Sullivan's architectural leadership during a European tour in 1914. When in 1916 the Sidney bank officials decided to construct a new building, Studevant went to Newark, Ohio, to examine Sullivan's design for the Home Building Association. This experience convinced him that Sullivan could help him fulfill his own City Beautiful ideals and his bank's progressive enterprises.[4] Sullivan's previous bank designs met Studevant's expectations for a new bank building that would combine beauty, public convenience, and advanced technology. In his 1918 review of the Sidney bank, Thomas Tallmadge credited Studevant with the idea that "a bank should be a financial service station, democratic in its accessibility to its officers and social in its supply of beauty and comfort to its patrons; as a service station it should be scientific and complete." He quoted Studevant as proclaiming, "Show me your ventilating system, and I will tell you how much your architect knows."[5]

Neither Studevant's recommendation nor Sullivan's preliminary schemes were immediately approved by the more conservative members of the building committee (figure 47). The story of Sullivan's initial visit to Sidney, first told by W. H. Wagner, then president of the bank,[6] records his spontaneity in composing the first—and usually the final—scheme after he had carefully studied the site and building program:

Sullivan retired to the opposite corner [of the building site], sat on a curbstone for the better part of two days, smoking innumerable cigarettes. Then at the end of that time, he announced to the directors that the design was made—in his head. He proceeded to rapidly draw a sketch for them, and announced an estimate of the cost.

Wagner's report also indicates the extent of Sullivan's self-image as a creator of a new, American style and the effacer of outworn historical forms. When Sullivan presented his sketches to the building committee,

one of the directors was somewhat disturbed by the unfamiliarity of the style, and suggested that he rather fancied some classic columns and pilasters for the facade. Sullivan very brusquely rolled up his sketch and started to depart, saying that the directors could get a thousand architects to design a classic bank but only one to design this kind of bank, and that as far as he was concerned it was one or the other.[7]

It is not known at what point during these discussions Studevant's opinion prevailed. But soon after 8 May 1917, Sullivan had sent blueprints to his new clients; the building project was completed almost exactly one year later.

The building site remains one of the most prominent locations in downtown Sidney, which is laid out on a gridiron plan with a massive, ornate Second Empire style courthouse at its center. The Sidney bank site is on the corner of one of six streets that lead to Courthouse Square. (For the new building, the bank owners demolished the nineteenth-century commercial building in which they had previously rented space.)

As in Newark, Sullivan encountered reddish brick-faced Italianate commercial buildings that extend the bold architectural modeling of the courthouse elevations. Heavily bracketed cornices and segmental or half-circle arched windows and doorways give this town center both unity and picturesque variety. Sullivan preserved and reordered these indigenous patterns, demonstrating again that a modern style of architecture can be both continuous with and distinct from historical styles. As in Newark, Grinnell, and Owatonna, he made the rectangular mass of the bank a terminus and an anchor for an irregular accretion of facades and building heights. Here, too, he subdivided the mass with simple geometry: for the main elevation he inscribed a half-circle within a square (figure 47), and for the side elevation he delineated verticals and horizontals as an abstraction of support and span. Furthermore, he made bolder both the primary architectonic forms and his own organic ornamental relief.[8]

The increased scale and plasticity of Sullivan's ornament in relation to mass can best be explained as an attempt to redefine the prevailing systems of architectural decoration in the neighboring civic monuments.[9] Much like the courthouse in Newark, Sidney's Shelby County Courthouse is faced with greenish-gray limestone and light buff sandstone classical motifs. The three-story elevations of a Greek cross plan are boldly adorned with columns, pediments, and sculptural reliefs. A central clock tower gives a vertical accent to the whole. In responding to the courthouse composition, Sullivan did not simply repeat the solution he had arrived at for the Newark bank. His response indicates how he solved "a particular problem for its own purpose."[10] In Sidney, a Gothic revival style building, the Monumental Building located catercorner with the bank, forced Sullivan to reconsider the didactic function of his medium and means of representation: tinted brick, marble, mosiac, and terra cotta.

The Monumental Building imposes on Sidney a strong historical and architectural presence. Erected in 1875 to commemorate the town's Civil War soldiers, it originally housed a public library and opera house in the upper three floors and a row of stores on the ground floor. In its midwestern setting, the Monumental Building is an unusual but good example of the Gothic revival style. Venetian or Ruskinian Gothic revival motifs, executed in light sandstone, enhance the flat red brick surfaces and the vertical dimensions of the four-story elevations. Sullivan denounced such revival style buildings and would have considered the Monumental Building typical of the era's misuse of historical architectural forms. Sullivan argued that ornament borrowed from the past (and "stuck on") lacked organic integrity with both the life of the building and the life of the American people. He tried to correct these aberrations by showing that a new mode of ornament, derived from nature rather than outmoded styles, should be correlated with the functional mass, construction, and naturalistic color scheme of the structure.

In his review of the Sidney bank, Tallmadge addressed just such formal problems to explain how Sullivan successfully integrated art and utility. Tallmadge praised the Sidney bank as a further refinement of Sullivan's solution for the rural bank, calling it one of the most brilliant "gems . . . on a necklace of latter-day achievement, headed by the epoch-making Owatonna Bank" (plates 10, 11).[11] He observed Sullivan's skill in using ordinary materials as a "palette" of colors and tones to modulate high and low relief and solids and voids with the surfaces of the mass. Tallmadge extended his artistic metaphors for Sullivan's banks when he analyzed the sequence of colors used for the exterior glazed reliefs and

"tapestry" or tinted brick. He described how mottled turtle green passes through brown and tan and then "becomes lighter until it emerges into golden hues in the frame of the great window of the side [elevation], and dies into pale orange in the cornices."[12]

Sullivan varied these color tones to augment the natural effects of highlights and shadows. He used lighter tones for high relief and projecting surfaces and darker tones for low relief and receding surfaces. He also mixed the warm values of the terra cotta reliefs with those of natural sunlight to enhance the colors and textures of fourteen shades of roughcut tinted brick. By setting this glowing, golden-reddish mass on a base of richly veined dark green marble, he contrasted and intensified complementary hues and tones to create a chromatic harmony throughout the whole. Above the "great window," Sullivan reordered the dominant colors of his palette; he inserted into the brick wall a green mosaic panel as a scintillating field for the gold tile inscription of the bank's name.

Early twentieth-century critics considered the formal elements an architect used for compositional unity fundamental to making utility artistic. Tallmadge admired three such elements in the Sidney bank elevations—the cornice, the entrance door and its mosaic tympanum, and the "great window."

Tallmadge commended both the "designer and fabricator"[13] for the terra cotta reliefs. He considered the cornice relief a triumph of design (as a unifying element) as well as a triumph of execution. In the cornice and in the entrance door enframement he observed an "organic" integrity between the relief ornament and the building's mass and substance. These reliefs reveal the modeling and casting of terra cotta and exhibit those clay-like properties terra cotta shares with brick. Tallmadge noted that in the broad, "beautiful" arch over the doorway, the "considerable projection and enriched soffits" hold in place "the magnificent tympanum in glass mosaic" (plate 12). In this mosaic, executed by Louis J. Millet, the gold letters of "Thrift" are embedded in a brilliant field of turquoise blue and framed by two-dimensional, geometric translations of Sullivan's relief ornament. Mosaic arabesques of violet, orange-brown, yellow, and green produce brilliant chromatic harmonies and make the panel fluctuate between projection and recession. These abstract chromatic patterns create an illusion of shifting highlights and shadows continuous with those nuances of the framing three-dimensional relief. Viewed together, the arch and tympanum motif dissolve and activate both the surface and mass.

Finally, Tallmadge regarded the "extraordinary range of windows that illuminate the main banking room" as the most "brilliant" feature of the whole exterior. Calling this masterful window arrangement "unprecedented," he pointed to its full range of "modeling and rich color." He especially admired the projecting corbels under the window mullions, which can be read as supports that are gradually modeled onto the surface. Tallmadge also appreciated how the gradation of hues within the window framework conforms with the highlights and shadows of the overall mass.[14]

Tallmadge's observations and Sullivan's own statements indicate how early twentieth-century architects and critics addressed the problem of reconciling aesthetic standards derived from masonry construction with the new building technologies of reinforced concrete and steel. Tallmadge applied to the "reeded" window mullions and the escutcheon over the mosaic panel the compositional norms for gradations between ornament and mass or between solids and voids. He found both these features lacking the subtle sculptural and chromatic transitions he ad-

mired in the window corbels and the entrance arch reliefs. At first, Tallmadge reacted in a similar way to the relief motifs over the four small, rectangular windows at each corner of the elevations. Later he recognized that he had erroneously used "old standards" to analyze the relationship between solids and voids, what he described as "the huge beautifully modeled terra cotta broaches that pin the lacelike window trim to the brick fabric [and the] void of the unornamented small windows." His reevaluation occurred after he asked Sullivan to "justify himself." Sullivan responded, "Every schoolboy knows there is steel over those windows." Tallmadge concluded from this "modern" perspective of construction and design that the broaches and window voids "looked all right."[15]

The contrast between ornament and void in the whole scheme can also be read in strictly formal terms and in accordance with Sullivan's personal symbolism. First, Sullivan superimposed ornament on the void to set up and then to resolve a surface tension that enlivens the entire composition. While the organic flourish contrasts with the rendered rectangular void, these elements are equally proportioned in order to dynamically balance each other. Second, Sullivan symbolized the complementary relationships between ornament as the emotional-subjective expression of art and geometry as the logical-objective expression of necessity. The second reading converges with the first; we can also read the ornamental motif as pointing to the source of illumination for interior spaces partitioned off from the main banking hall.

In the interior of the Peoples Savings and Loan Association building, Sullivan realized most fully the practical and symbolic aspects of the democratic plan (figures 48a, 49). As in the Cedar Rapids, Grinnell, and Newark banks, he continued to use polished plate glass partitions and

46
Peoples Savings and Loan Association, Sidney, Ohio, 1916–18. Photo: Henry Fuermann, Chicago Architectural Photographing Co.

47
Peoples Savings and Loan Association, preliminary drawing of main elevation, 15 December 1916. Photograph (location of drawing unknown).

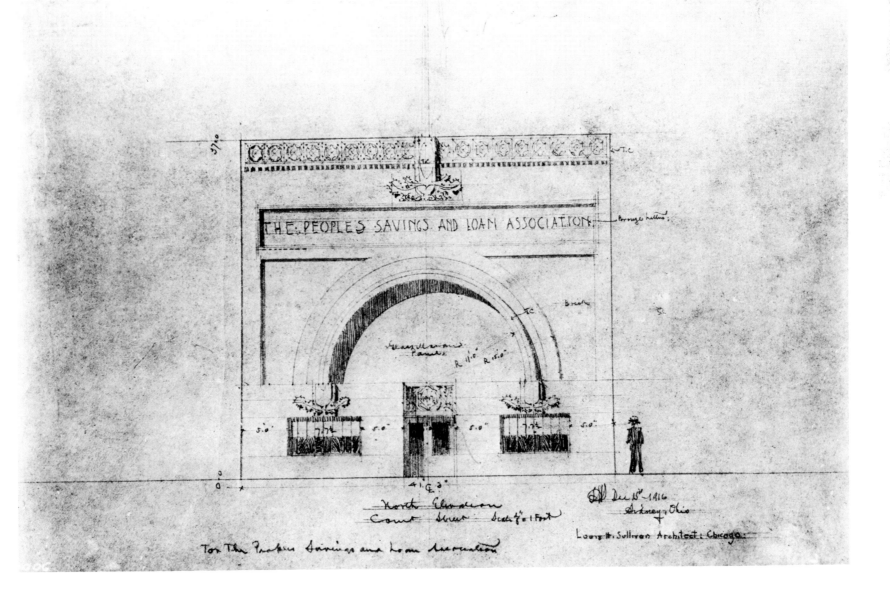

48a
Peoples Savings and Loan Association, view toward closed vault. Photo: Henry Fuermann, Chicago Architectural Photographing Co.

48b
Peoples Savings and Loan Association, view toward open vault. Photo: Lauren S. Weingarden.

49
Peoples Savings and Loan Association, main floor and upper level plans. Reprinted from *American Architect* 64 (23 October 1918): plate 124.

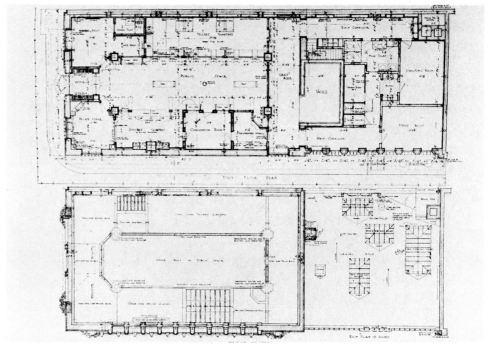

open counter tops between the main banking space and the tellers' cages and stenographers' and officers' quarters. But here Sullivan extended a continuous glass partition between two corner piers at the rear of the banking hall to enhance the visual immediacy of the open layout—an effect to which all other features cohere.

Upon entering the banking room from the vestibule, the spectator/user has an unobstructed view of the open vault door, located at the end of the central axis (figure 48b). Sullivan delineated the orthogonals of a one-point perspective toward the open vault door with orthogonals formed by the regular sequence of square brick piers. He further emphasized this focal point with a continuous architrave, which, carried by the piers, forms a frame for the transparent wall. At floor level, Sullivan redefined the central axis by aligning a water fountain with two marble benches. He then turned the horizontal into a vertical axis and marked this perpendicular with a relief-framed bronze clock that crowns both the axis and architrave.

Tallmadge's description of the interior suggests two ways to experience the open layout. To the untutored eye, the direct view of the open vault corroborated the popular notion of the bank as a place of safekeeping. Tallmadge suggested this association when he described "the great vault door, which when open . . . forms its own picture—an apotheosis of polished steel and brass."[16] Local observers endorsed this practical, albeit mundane, analogy between the vault's function and its location. As one local historian wrote: "In the central perspective the greater circular door of the safe deposit vault, almost overpowering in its invincibility and strength, seems to set the seal of absolute completeness on the whole."[17] But Tallmadge, well aware of Sullivan's nonutilitarian metaphors, explained the second way of experiencing the interior. He

described how the visual climax of the vault signified Sullivan's achievement in rendering the mechanistic artistic:

The extraordinary harmony of Mr. Sullivan's architecture, with so final an expression of mechanical skill and untrammeled modernity as this vault door, is deeply significant. It tells that machinery and art greet each other with open arms where there is mutual understanding.[18]

Sullivan further unified the interior space with abstract elements of design (figures 48a, 50; plate 13). He redefined a theme of rectilineation, derived from the rectangular mass, with the straight lines and right angles of structural elements, furniture, and carved and cast ornamental reliefs. Built-in marble desks and counter tops, quarter-sawn oak Craftsman-style cabinets and woodwork, and even the rectangular patterns of the opalescent glass windows reinforce an image of "simplicity itself."[19]

With natural materials and chromatic lighting, Sullivan avoided an image of austere, mechanistic precision. He combined the warm, neutral brown tones of stained wood, glazed reliefs (cf. figure 4), and salt-fired glazed Roman brick with the complementary colors of pinkish-gray Tennessee marble floors and antique verde marble counters and desk tops. Sullivan then illuminated the whole interior with the soft, warm radiance of colored light filtered through the opalescent blue skylight and nine leaded glass windows on the west elevation. In this open expanse of the wall, brilliant red, green, and yellow rectangular patterns are set within fields of mottled blue and yellow-ochre. Electric light, originally emitted from bulbs clustered in urns above the corner piers and from troughs above the architrave, combined with natural light to produce an even glow, in which, as Tallmadge observed, there "are no shadows or highlights."[20]

Later observers have admired the restrained simplicity of the bank's interior, and some have praised especially the elements of reductivist design in the south elevation clerestory.[21] However, contemporary records, including Tallmadge's review, indicate that mural paintings or fresco decorations had been planned but were postponed—and, consequently, were never executed—due to the wartime economy.[22] Such reports clarify two forgotten facts. First, Sullivan considered his interior designs complete only with the application of such naturalistic schemes. Second, he did not intend his interiors to be as austere as his later admirers believed. A contemporary viewer described an experience of the interior that is more consistent with Sullivan's efforts to compensate for the "incomplete" state of the interior. This Sidney journalist wrote about the luminous chromatic effects that both facilitate practical work and ensure an artistic event. He observed:

The lighting, by means of the great mullioned window on the west, and the beautiful roof light, is perfectly toned to relieve the eye of strain and in no single corner of the banking department is there any shadow, nor any glare. Not by accident is this result attained, but by the applied science of the artist and architect. The artificial lighting is equally perfect and beautiful in visual effect. *Simplicity is striking throughout the interior, but every surface is rich in softened beauty of tone and material* (emphasis added).[23]

A community meeting room, to be located in the basement of the bank, was yet another casualty of the wartime economy. Designed to fulfill the bank's function as "a social as well as financial center" of Sidney, it was just one of the practical and technological features Sullivan introduced to meet modern banking needs. As in the banks in Owatonna, Cedar Rapids, Grinnell, and Newark, the Sidney bank allotted a separate banking room to its women patrons (figure 51). Adjacent to the vestibule,

the women's room balanced the size and place of the office in the opposite southeast corner. While the women's room was open to the main banking room from above, at ground story it was completely closed off. Conversely, the office on the other side of the entrance was sealed above with a wood ceiling but could be opened or closed to the officers' quarters with a sliding wood partition. The men's room, director's office, board room, and the coupon room comprised the remainder of the space in the annex behind the main banking room. Sullivan paid no less attention to detail in the secondary spaces than he did in the more public areas. He lined the offices, the tellers' cages, secretarial quarters, and corridors with built-in Craftsman-style storage units and illuminated each of these spaces with their own skylights (figure 50).

Bank officials could also tout a variety of technological novelties. For example, a stenographer, seated in the office next to the mechanized vault, operated an automatic lock to admit bank patrons and employees through the glass partition into the vault area. As the Studevant remark quoted at the beginning of this section suggests, Sullivan's clients in Sidney most often praised his scheme for heating, cooling, and ventilating. This system, together with double-glazed windows, controlled the temperature of the hermetically sealed building. Heating and cooling were operated by "vapor modulation" of recycled "washed air" that passed through a series of heating coils which, in turn, automatically adjusted temperatures to the changing seasons. (As in some of his other banks, Sullivan forced ventilated air through shafts inside structural piers, a technique he had developed in the skyscrapers.) When it was first introduced, this network of vents and blowers was lauded for its "noiseless and dustless" operation; later, it was easily adapted to a modern air-conditioning system.

50
Peoples Savings and Loan Association, view toward officers' quarters and clere-story windows. Photo: Henry Fuermann, Chicago Architectural Photographing Co.

51
Peoples Savings and Loan Association, women's room. Photo: Henry Fuermann, Chicago Architectural Photographing Co.

Shortly after the Peoples Savings and Loan Association building was completed, conservative bank officials were still skeptical about the economical wisdom of building such a novel structure. During one of the first meetings in the new board room, some members accused the majority of "acting hastily in demolishing the perfectly sound Robertson Building" and in "bringing in that revolutionary Chicago architect [to erect] a building in a new fangled style using too expensive materials."[24] In the following months, the shock of the new subsided. After actually working in the bank, the skeptics were finally convinced of Sullivan's expertise in efficient building, planning, and image-making. A 1919 text documents Sullivan's success. Here a local historian reviewed the impact of novel architecture on the bank's prosperity and, in turn, on Sidney's collective morality. This writer confirmed the popular opinion that economic and social amelioration was commensurate with an architectural imagery that joined modern technology with art. He wrote:

If so much space has been given to the little building that glows like a jewel on its much mooted corner, it is because it marks a departure from the day of mere utilitarianism and mistaken economy, which may, and it is to be hoped, will influence the future of Sidney. Already, the question "will it pay?" has been answered. Six, nearly seven times the cost of the building has been added to the deposits of the Association, which passed the three million mark some time ago.[25]

When the new Peoples Savings and Loan Association building opened, Sullivan helped to establish the connotations that the public derived from his architectural imagery. In a description of the bank printed in the *Sidney Daily News*, Sullivan promoted the pragmatist idea that the spiritual, moral, physical, and intellectual growth of the individual contributed to the well-being of society at large. He explained that the new, democratic architecture of the Sidney bank signified internal values ex-ternalized by social action. Here Sullivan alluded to the contrast between Sidney's archaic civic monuments and his own design. He insisted that he derived his innovative architectural forms from "the realities of life," rather than from "a mere decoration or veneer . . . of historical forms."[26]

Notes

1.

Sprague dates the first working drawing 11 April 1916; see "Sullivan and his Chief Draftsmen," p. 434.

2.

Morrison, *Louis Sullivan*, p. 220.

3.

Careful renovations were carried out by Sidney architect and preservationist Ferdinand E. Freytag. Mr. Freytag generously shared his time, expertise, and the bank's and his personal archives with me in June 1984. With Freytag's assistance, the bank has preserved the original blueprints and obsolete furniture, brick, and cast ornament, some of which will be displayed in an exhibition room designed specifically for their Sullivan collection. The bank has also published a commemorative booklet documenting the building history of Sullivan's project. See "Historical Sketches of Peoples Federal Savings and Loan Association, Sidney, Ohio," n.d. Unless otherwise noted, the following synopsis of the conditions of the commission are taken from this source.

4.

By 1916 the Peoples Savings and Loan Association had gained regional prominence over a thirty-year period because of its rapid growth, prosperity, and creative financing; see "The Story of Shelby County," in *Memoirs of Miami Valley*, eds. John C. Hover [et al.] (Chicago: R. O. Law & Co., 1919), pp. 402–5.

5.

Tallmadge, "The Peoples Savings and Loan Association," 480.

6.

This account is also provided by Connely, *Louis Sullivan*, p. 268.

7.

Quoted from the bank's "Historical Sketches." Morrison repeated this anecdote to characterize Sullivan's "mode of procedure"; see *Louis Sullivan*, p. 180.

8.

Sprague attributes the detailing of ornament to Parker N. Berry (who left Sullivan's office before the completion of this building); see "Sullivan and his Chief Draftsmen," pp. 156–57; cf. figure 4 above.

9.

To later critics treating the Sidney bank as a self-contained whole or viewing it in black-and-white photographs, the elevations appeared disproportionate and unresolved; see, for example, Morrison, *Louis Sullivan*, pp. 221–22.

10.

Rebori, "An Architecture of Democracy," 456.

11.

Tallmadge, "The Peoples Savings and Loan Association," 482.

12.

Ibid., 179. Tallmadge seems to have coined the term "tapestry" brick to describe Sullivan's use of tinted pressed brick; the term may have been derived from Sullivan's analogies between this brickwork and oriental tapestries; see Sullivan, "Artistic Brickwork."

13.

Ibid., 478. Tallmadge identified Mr. Gates of the American Terra Cotta Company as the "fabricator" and credited Louis J. Millet with the mosaic tympanum. However, we know that at this time Kristian Schneider (who was also in a partnership with Henry F. Erby) was chief modeler at the American Terra Cotta Company, which William D. Gates owned; therefore, Schneider should be identified as the "fabricator." See Reinhart, "Kristian Schneider," 12.

14.

Ibid., 479.

15.

Ibid. Tallmadge's anecdote gives us access to early twentieth-century aesthetics and enables us to shift our critical position from a later view, one that would require an exterior form to represent the underlying steel beam. Sullivan, like Tallmadge, joined progressive nineteenth-century rationalist standards with earlier conventions for reading the architectonic and even metaphorical qualities of the wall surface. On the one hand, they sanctioned "modern" steel construction for its structural minima. On the other hand, they exploited the non-loadbearing wall provided by the steel skeleton to compose the wall surface abstractly, as if it were a picture plane.

Blueprints show in detail a section of the enframed window, where a steel beam runs horizontally under the window frame and is attached to vertical I-beams in the window piers, including the mullions framing the ends.

16.

Ibid., 480.

17.

"The Story of Shelby County," *Memoirs of the Miami Valley*, p. 405.

18.

Tallmadge, "The Peoples Savings and Loan Association," 480.

19.

Ibid., 479.

20.

Ibid., 481.

21.

See, for example, Morrison, *Louis Sullivan*, p. 222.

22.

Tallmadge, "The Peoples Savings and Loan Association," 480; see also, "Peoples Savings and Loan Association Opening," *The Sidney Daily News*, 26.

23.

Ibid.

24.

Cited from bank pamphlet, "Historical Sketches."

25.

"The Story of Shelby County," *Memoirs of the Miami Valley*, p. 405.

26.

Although not signed by Sullivan, a pragmatist tract on "democratic art" following a description of the bank is strongly suggestive of his writing style, vocabulary, and theory at this time; see "Peoples Savings and Loan Association Opening," *The Sidney Daily News*, 26.

N.W. corner James and Broadway (now Dickason) Streets

Columbus, Wisconsin

Dates

Preliminary sketches:

15 February 1919 (plans; "redrawn" 24 February)

22 February 1919 (revisions for facade and side elevation)

26 February 1919 (facade)

Final drawings:

24 March 1919 (plans; "corrected" 31 March)

14, 16 April 1919 (sections)[1]

Official opening: 14 June 1920

Addition: 1961

Sullivan was fortunate to have sympathetic and artistically informed clients for his last two bank commissions. John Russell Wheeler, president of the Farmers and Merchants National Bank, like LaFayette Studevant, provided collegial as well as financial support. But unlike Studevant, who from the outset was an advocate of Sullivan's modernism, Wheeler originally was an adversary of progressive architecture.

In his own account of his conversion from traditionalism to modernism, Wheeler recalled that he endorsed Sullivan's total architectural scheme only after he proved that he could fulfill the bank's practical demands. Wheeler had researched modern banking facilities for several years, and when he concluded his study, he decided to finance personally any costs that exceeded the bank's building budget. Then he began to look for an architect who could fit a modern bank into a traditional Greco-Roman temple form. He attributed his conversion to modernism in general and to Sullivan's modernism in particular to his wife. She persuaded him to visit Sullivan in Chicago and finally to commission Sullivan to design the new bank building. As Wheeler explained, his transition was a difficult one:

I was scared to death. . . . I was supposed to be a conservative man, a fairly distinguished member of a conservative profession and I was being asked to build a building that looked to me flamboyantly radical. And I was sure I would terrify the natives. . . . It was Mrs. Wheeler who soothed my feathers and talked me into going ahead.[2]

Sullivan's various sketches for elevations and plans confirm Wheeler's artistic uncertainties. During Sullivan's first visit to Columbus, toward the middle of February 1919, he proposed at least three designs for the main facade (figures 52–54), two preliminary designs for the side elevation (one facade design and one elevation design are marked "restudy,"

52
Farmers and Merchants Union Bank,
Columbus, Wisconsin, 1919–20. Detail,
preliminary drawing for main elevation,
15 February 1919. Pencil on paper. Avery
Library, Columbia University.

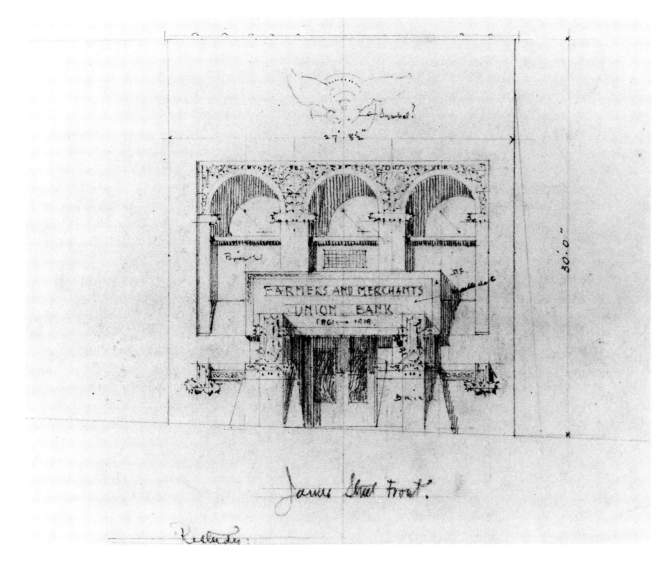

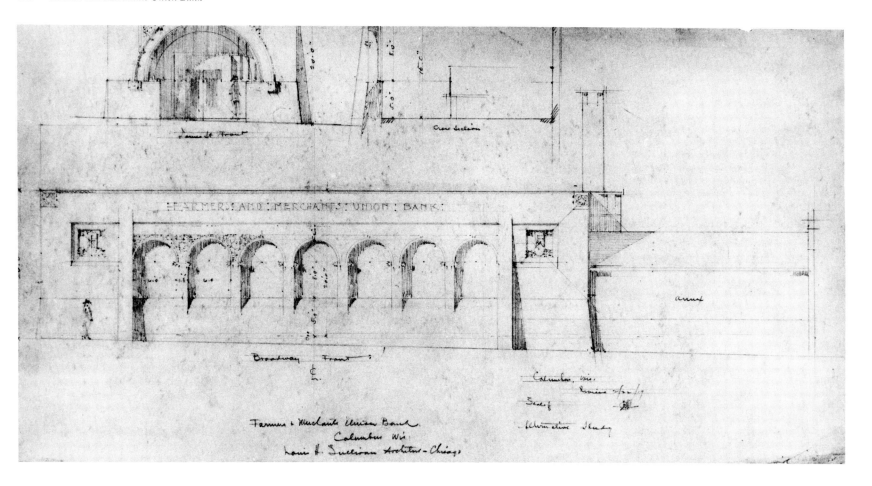

figure 54), and two alternative plans (figures 55, 56). Even the final plans underwent revisions between 24 and 31 March (figure 57).[3] The "FINAL" scheme for the front and side elevations is also dated 31 March (figure 58). Notwithstanding this laborious start, construction proceeded rapidly once Wheeler accepted the final designs. From then on, a friendly, personal relationship developed between the client and the architect.[4]

Wheeler thought that a modern bank should house both financial and social activities. He wanted his new bank to serve local businessmen and farmers as a meeting place and as a repository of information on agricultural research.[5] According to local journalists, Sullivan succeeded in giving the bank an image of financial security, civic monumentality, and community activity. One reporter described the bank as "beautiful and homelike,"[6] and another drew attention to its easy access from street level.[7] These views of the bank's aesthetic and domestic attributes resulted from at least two of Sullivan's inversions of the temple-form bank: he eliminated the podium and stairs leading to an elevated bank hall, and he replaced the highly finished white stones (or marble) of classicism with the textured, chromatic materials and organic ornament of naturalism.

One reporter, unusually attuned to the integrity and symbolism of the built townscape, noted that Sullivan's design asserted its individuality and yet harmonized with both the business district and the civic monuments it faced. This writer praised Sullivan for his firsthand analysis of the site and of the special functions of the small town bank. He noted that Sullivan

came to [study] the environment of the proposed building, realizing that such a structure must harmonize not alone with its purposes and uses

55
Farmers and Merchants Union Bank, preliminary plan of main floor, 15 February 1919, revised 24 February 1919. Pencil on paper. Avery Library, Columbia University.

56
Farmers and Merchants Union Bank, preliminary plan of main floor, 15 February 1919. Pencil on paper. Avery Library, Columbia University.

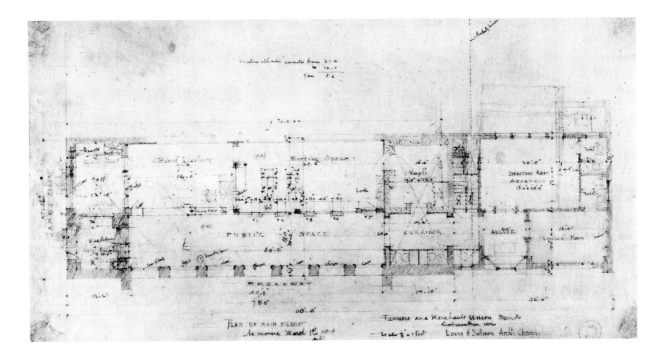

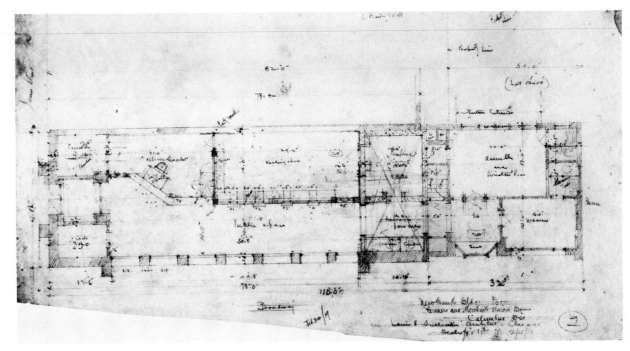

57
**Farmers and Merchants Union Bank, plan
of main floor, 24 March 1919, "corrected"
31 March 1919. Pencil on paper. Avery
Library, Columbia University.**

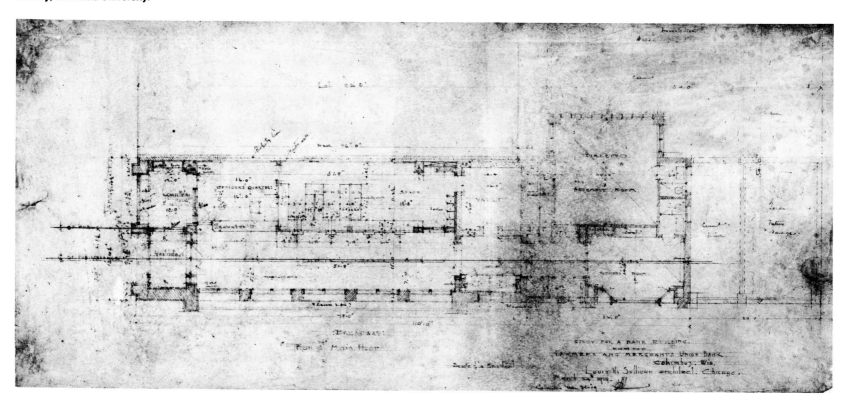

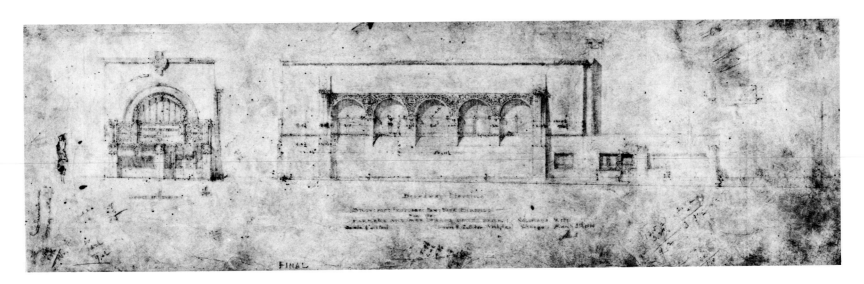

58
Farmers and Merchants Union Bank,
"FINAL" main and east elevations, 31
March 1919. Pencil on paper. Avery
Library, Columbia University.

but as a place of business, and with the plans and ideas of the builders, but also with the space to be occupied and with the surroundings.

With these conditions fulfilled, the writer considered Sullivan's overall achievement:

The bank's location is exceptional not alone in the fact that the main current of the city's life touches it constantly but in the farther fact that this outlook commands wide spaces, and that it has a certain definiteness and individuality of place without losing any of that close contact with the environment.[8]

Sullivan responded to the built environment by creating for the Farmers and Merchants Union Bank one of his most picturesque and sculptural bank designs. The bank is located at the intersection of two major streets that separate the civic from the commercial life of Columbus. It occupies the northwest corner of James and Dickason (formerly Broadway) streets and provides a visual terminus for the commercial buildings along this north-west axis. Across Dickason, the bank faces another domestic-like design for a public building. The public library, completed in 1911, evokes Prairie School domestic architecture with its low, broad overhanging gabled roofs and lightly colored cubic masses.[9] At the southeast corner of the intersection, the bank faces the 1892 city hall. This structure is everything the library is not. It is executed in red brick with yellow sandstone trim and features the more vertical, ponderous, and picturesque massing of the Romanesque revival style.

Sullivan's revised studies for the elevations incorporate abstract elements from his client's idea of a classical temple-form bank, from the existing medieval revival style, and from the more recent simple forms of an indigenous style. He reduced the structural elements and simplified the proportions derived from this historical lineage to what he considered timeless, universal forms. He thus synthesized the statics and objective, logical forms of classicism and the dynamics and subjective, emotional forms of the medieval style. He further emphasized the abstract forms and massing of prairie architecture.[10]

Sullivan's designs for the Columbus bank elevations illustrate how he abstracted the pier, lintel, and arch—"the letters of our [architectural] alphabet"—to articulate structural facts and organic metaphors. Two studies for the main elevation show medieval and classical alternatives (figures 52, 54). In one, he made the entrance into a low, broad Richardsonian Romanesque arch that springs from battered imposts and outside the square frame (figure 54).[11] In the other, he reduced the arch to a semicircle within a square (figure 52), a solution reminiscent of the main facade of the Sidney bank (figure 47; plate 10). Here he reinforced these reductivist classical forms with the more attenuated, Order-like proportions of framing pilasters (capped by shield-bearing winged lions). In another "restudy" Sullivan superimposed a three-part arcade on an entrance enframed by a pier and lintel motif (figure 53). This solution recalls his skyscraper designs, the annex elevations at the Owatonna bank (figure 7), and, possibly, his first design for that bank's main block.

The "final" drawing for the main facade best illustrates Sullivan's design process (figure 58). He first abstracted the pier, lintel, and arch into horizontals, verticals, and half-circles and then arranged these elements according to simple arithmetic proportions (here in 1:2 ratios). Next, he enlivened these geometric elements with his organic mode of ornament—his own analogues to objective classical and subjective medieval means of representation.[12] In the completed facade, Sullivan combined the picturesque variety of the city hall and the simple massing and wall piers of the library with the geometric order of his own most abstract studies. The entrance shows another timeless, objective means Sullivan employed to order the whole; he used the arithmetic proportions and geometric figures to make an asymmetrical entrance appear symmetrical.

In the "final" drawing and completed version of the side or Dickason elevation, Sullivan transformed medieval battered wall buttresses for modern re-use (figures 58, 59). The buttresses have a formal function; they frame the recessed arcades of stained glass windows. These buttresses are also structural facts; like the piers of the window arcade, they support steel I-beams that span the ceiling of the main banking room (figures 60–62). Sullivan varied the dimensions and modeling of the piers in relation to both structure and surface. He reduced the piers to simple vertical posts to designate their structural function. Since the two outer piers frame the window arcade, Sullivan projected these members from the wall. In contrast, he modulated the window arcade piers into the planar brick surface to emphasize the pictorial quality of the multicolored leaded glass and surrounding light green terra cotta reliefs (plate 14).

Thomas Tallmadge considered the Columbus bank second only to the Owatonna bank.[13] He especially admired Sullivan's achievements as a modeler of terra cotta[14] and praised the subtle sculptural transitions between relief ornament and the surface of the rectangular mass for relieving stasis or augmenting the "motion" of the building. Tallmadge observed in the main elevation a modeling technique similar to that used in the side elevation. In the outer frame of the arch, brick soffits recede in two stages, repeating the light and shade patterns of the low-relief inner frame (figure 63).[15]

Celebrating the Farmers and Merchants Union Bank as "a gorgeous butterfly against its cemented and white neighbors," Tallmadge paid tribute to Sullivan's efforts to embellish the rural townscape with his paint-

erly palette. He described how Sullivan used "tapestry brick," with shades ranging from brown to gold, to produce a "richness and prismatic lustre" of reddish hues. Here, as in his previous banks, Sullivan introduced shades of green to attain chromatic harmony through the simultaneous contrast of complementary colors. For the terra cotta reliefs of this exterior, he used a single shade of mottled green matte glaze (plate 14). He enhanced the general polychromatic theme by inserting above the entrance a deep green marble plaque inscribed with the gilded letters of his own name and that of the bank.

Sullivan repeated the geometric and chromatic elements of the exterior composition—circles, squares, and rectangles cast in red and green hues—throughout the interior. Again assisted by Louis J. Millet, Sullivan established the dominant color tones in the geometric patterns of the leaded glass windows. For the tympanum window he rendered these motifs in complementary color combinations of red and green and of orange and blue stained glass and set them against a field of mottled blue and green opalescent glass. In the windows of the Dickason Street elevation, Sullivan extended his chromatic palette to include the paler tones of the dominant hues. He used Craftsman-style woodwork, finished with a greenish-gray stain, and speckled, light brown Roman brick to associate the decorative scheme with the colors of nature (figures 60, 64, 65). This association is especially effective when these surfaces are bathed in a warm golden glow produced by the blending of diffused chromatic light (plate 15).

Sullivan's clients rejected his proposal for a skylight over the main banking area. But when he modified his democratic plan, he typically accommodated both their practical and social needs. Sullivan moved the entrance and major axis from the center to the east side of the building

59
Farmers and Merchants Union Bank.
Photo: Henry Fuermann, Chicago
Architectural Photographing Co.

60
Farmers and Merchants Union Bank, view
of public space toward rear. Photo: Henry
Fuermann, Chicago Architectural Photo-
graphing Co.

61
Farmers and Merchants Union Bank, longitudinal section looking north, 16 April 1919. Pencil on paper. Avery Library, Columbia University.

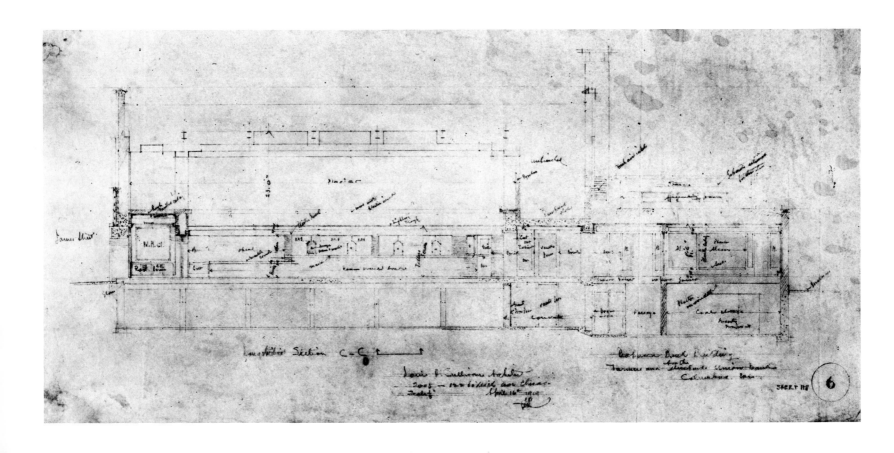

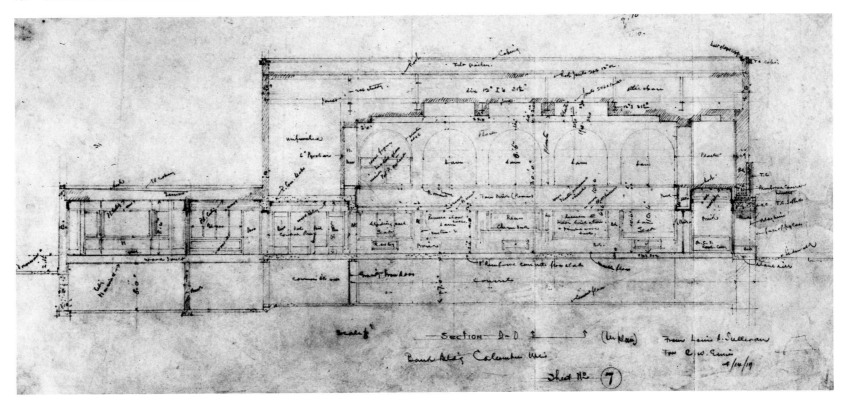

62
Farmers and Merchants Union Bank, longitudinal section looking south, 14 April 1919. Pencil on paper. Avery Library, Columbia University.

63
Farmers and Merchants Union Bank, main facade. Photo: Henry Fuermann, Chicago Architectural Photographing Co.

64
Farmers and Merchants Union Bank, view of tellers' space, officers' quarters, consultation room, vestibule. Courtesy of Farmers and Merchants Union Bank.

65
Farmers and Merchants Union Bank, meeting room. Courtesy of Farmers and Merchants Union Bank.

in order to provide the main banking space and tellers' cages with direct, natural light from the east wall windows.[16] He left counter tops open and used glass partitions to make visible the officers' quarters and tellers' areas located along the west side of the building (figures 60, 64). The open vault was not visible for public display. Instead, Sullivan enclosed the vault in a space parallel to the major axis that forms a corridor aligning the main entrance with the annex (figure 57).

Sullivan also adapted his modified democratic plan to the community services Wheeler considered essential to his bank. The asymmetrical axis calls attention to other practical functions of the democratic layout, some of which are unique to this bank. For example, with the axial corridor, Sullivan emphasized the public accessibility to the director's office and community assembly room in the annex (figure 65). He also gave the annex visual and functional distinction with a separate entrance on the west elevation and with a more domestic scale and ambience (figure 59). In addition, Sullivan built book and display cases along the east walls of the axial passage, where Wheeler posted the latest information regarding agricultural research and financing (figure 60).

Finally, in this corridor and behind the vault, Sullivan placed a stairway that leads to a balcony or mezzanine. Marked "unfinished" in the preliminary and working drawings, the balcony was to be used for additional work space (figure 61). Whatever the intended function, from this elevated position one gains a complete overview of the open plan and banking activities. From here one also has a full view of the vividly colored windows and the play of their reflected colors on the plain, unadorned surfaces of the beamed ceiling and the west clerestory wall. Today we can still take an unexpected visual delight in these brilliant, scintillating nuances, an optical experience that a local journalist first discovered as

he stood in the balcony just after the bank was completed.

In his review of the bank, this same journalist summarized the "main purposes" of the bank's builder and the first impressions of visitors to the bank. He restated the builder's three-fold objective that the bank "should be an inspiration for better bank architecture; that it might serve as an example of what a country bank should be; [and] that it might be a service center for the community, exemplifying the best and broadest ideas of modern banking." And he recorded the words of praise spoken by the many bankers who had visited the Columbus bank: "No Space Wasted!" "Nothing Crowded!" "Nothing Left Out!" "Beautiful."[17]

While neither Sullivan nor his reviewer knew that the Columbus bank would be his last completed bank design, these remarks might well serve as an epitaph to Sullivan's brilliant yet sporadic career as a master designer of rural town banks and as a master image-maker for democracy. With these banks Sullivan renewed Emerson's prospects for a truly American art form. In addition to beautifying utility, he realigned the mechanical arts with nature, making architecture a fine art and, consequently, a means for realigning humanity with nature.

Notes

1.
All dates derived from a folio of fourteen drawings for Farmers and Merchants Union Bank in the Avery Library, Columbia University. This folio was a gift to the Avery Library from George Grant Elmslie in 1936.

2.
Quoted from John Szarkowski, *The Idea of Louis Sullivan* (Minneapolis: University of Minnesota Press, 1956), p. 5. Wheeler preserved the blueprints and other documents relating to Sullivan's work on the bank. These documents are on view in the exhibition area of the bank, in the mezzanine or balcony overlooking the banking hall.

3.
Plan dated 15, 24 February (figure 55) corresponds with elevation marked "restudy" of 26 February (figure 53, which is only a fragment of the complete sheet, which includes a cross section). The elevation dated 15 February (figure 52) and an "alternative study" (figure 54) were designed for another plan dated 15 February (figure 56). This latter plan is unusual among Sullivan's bank layouts; the vestibule is oblong with exedrae at either end. It is reminiscent of what I believe to be Berry's Algona scheme, where there is both an alcove and a vestibule.

4.
For accounts of the Sullivan and Wheeler collaboration, see Joan Saltzman, "Bank A Glowing Jewel Box," *Milwaukee Sentinel* (12 May 1966): 1 ("Modern Living Section"); "Farmers & Merchants Union Bank 100th Anniversary Edition: 1861–1961," *The Columbus Journal-Republic* (31 August 1961). Saltzman reports that Wheeler's daughter remembered Sullivan's visits with

pleasure; she writes: "The architect was a gallant and dapper man . . . contrary to stories of his excesses at that time. And he was a delightful house guest."

5.
One of the first plans (figure 55) includes a library along the west wall and behind the open-countered officers' space.

6.
"Opening Day at F. & M. Union Bank," *The Columbus Republican* (19 June 1920): 1.

7.
"New Bank Building Constructed" (a review dated 1919–1920 and reprinted in "Farmers & Merchants Union Bank 100th Anniversary Edition").

8.
Ibid. Sullivan, a frequent visitor to Columbus, may have written these objectives for the press or stated them in a personal interview with the reporter. Following the passage cited here, Sullivan asserted the equal importance of meeting the bank client's practical needs. This statement is similar to Sullivan's 1918 letter to a prospective banker client in Winterset, Iowa; cited (without source reference) in Lathrop, "The Prairie School Bank," 56.

9.
The Columbus Public Library, designed by Claude and Starck, is illustrated and briefly discussed by Gordon D. Orr, Jr., "Louis W. Claude: Madison Architect of the Prairie School," *The Prairie School Review* 14 (Final Issue): 17.

10.
See, for example, Sullivan, "Emotional Architecture as Compared with Intellectual," 200; and the introductory essay above.

11.
In both this Richardsonian design and the more abstract classical versions, Sullivan recalls his own architectural past (and, in turn, that of the Prairie School) with allusions to such works as the Auditorium Building, the Walker Warehouse, the Wainwright Tomb, and the Golden Doorway of the Transportation Building.

12.
A drawing for the Eliel Apartments (1894) also shows this process; see no. 79 in Sprague, *The Drawings of Louis Sullivan*.

Sullivan's drawing technique for the "final" scheme also illustrates the style of what Sprague has described as "the minutiae of dots and broken lines of Sullivan's mature period" (that is, dating from 1890); see Sprague, *The Drawings of Louis Sullivan*, pp. 7–8. This graphic stippling technique is similar to the optical blending of juxtaposed pigments that occurs in his fresco patterns. Thus, the graphic method results in an analogously conceived Impressionist effect; see my article, "The Colors of Nature," 257, note 30.

13.
Tallmadge, "The Farmers' and Merchants' Bank," 63–65.

14.
Here as elsewhere Kristian Schneider, working for the American Terra Cotta Company, actually modeled the clay for terra cotta casting from Sullivan's drawings. See Reinhart, "Kristian Schneider," 15.

Other manufacturers of decorative work include Mathews Brothers Manufacturing Co. for the woodwork and McClymont Marble Co. for the marblework; both were Milwaukee firms. See "Unusual Building was

Mr. Wheeler's Dream" in "Farmers & Merchants Union Bank 100th Anniversary Edition."

15.
The eagles centered in the cornices of the main and rear elevations were required by the clients; the eagle is the Wisconsin state bird, and "Forward" the state's motto. A photograph of this section of relief with American Terra Cotta modelers was published in *Common Clay* I, no. 3 (1920), a trade journal published by the American Terra Cotta Company.

16.
Author's notes from bank documents.

17.
Cited from "Unusual Building was Mr. Wheeler's Dream" in "Farmers & Merchants Union Bank 100th Anniversary Edition." Sullivan was also present at the opening, where "he most thoroughly enjoyed meeting the people and studying the psychological effect that, the visit thru the building, had upon people individually and collectively" ("Opening Day at F. & M. Union Bank").

Bibliography

Bibliographic Note

Since several recently published monographs provide definitive bibliographies for works on and by Sullivan, the following references pertain more specifically to the banks and to the literature I have used to interpret Sullivan's theory and practice. What follows is a brief review of those monographic studies on Sullivan that have treated the banks as part of Sullivan's complete oeuvre. Thereafter Sullivan's writings, secondary sources related to the banks in general, and more detailed works related to each bank building are entered under separate headings. (Local newspaper reports are listed in the notes for each bank.)

Later critics and historians followed Hugh Morrison's formal analyses of the banks in *Louis Sullivan: Prophet of Modern Architecture* (New York: W. W. Norton & Co., [1935]; rpt. 1962). They praised the banks—especially the first bank, the National Farmers' Bank—for their bold reductivist massing, unadorned planar surfaces, and structural severity. They read this functionalist imagery as evidence of Sullivan's prophetic modernism. Conversely, they despaired over what they saw as disproportion between the abstract masses and structural elements, the high relief and large scale of ornament.

Morrison inadvertently laid the groundwork for biographical readings of Sullivan's formal juxtapositions. Morrison dismissed current "legends" that Sullivan's late works resulted from professional decline caused by "personal degeneration." However, he attributed these formal incongruities "to Sullivan's innate tendency to burst out at times into overwrought lyricism." Hence, for Morrison, as for later critics, these flourishes undermined the functionalist gains Sullivan had attained in his last works. Those writing after Morrison perceived these lyrical outbursts as the romantic indulgences of an embittered genius who increasingly encountered professional and personal crises after 1895.

For examples of modernist and biographical treatments of the banks in the context of Sullivan's career, see: Albert Bush-Brown, *Louis Sullivan* (New York: George Brazillier, 1960); Willard Connely, *Louis Sullivan as He Lived: The Shaping of American Architecture* (New York: Horizon Press, 1960); and Narciso G. Menocal, *Architecture as Nature: The Transcendentalist Idea of Louis Sullivan* (Madison: University of Wisconsin Press, 1981). A somewhat different approach is taken by William H. Jordy in "Functionalism as Fact and Symbol: Louis Sullivan's Commercial Buildings, Tombs, and Banks," in Volume 3 of *American Buildings and their Architects: Progressive and Academic Ideals at the Turn of the Century* (Garden City, New York: Anchor Books, 1976). Jordy argues that, in the banks as in Sullivan's earlier works, abstract formal elements connote practical, tectonic functions as well as philosophical values.

Two comprehensive studies of Sullivan have appeared since I completed my manuscript. Robert C. Twombly's *Louis Sullivan: His Life and Work* (New York: Viking-Elisabeth Sifton Books, 1986) incorporates the banks into the general context of Sullivan's personal history and stylistic development. Following a chronological approach to Sullivan's works, Twombly treats the banks as "late works" and pays most attention to those banks that have been best preserved and documented—the Owatonna and Sidney banks. As a detailed study of one bank, Larry Millett's *The Curve of the Arch: The Story of Louis Sullivan's Owatonna Bank* (St. Paul: Minnesota Historical Society, 1985) is a model of its kind. By bringing together all available material on the National Farmers' Bank, he surveys its building history, the lives of the patron and architect(s), and the history of remodelings and renovations. Since I used many of the documents available to Twombly and Millett, some of our data and interpretations overlap.

Writings by Louis H. Sullivan

"The Modern Phase of Architecture." A letter to Max Dunning, secretary of the Chicago Architectural Club, read in Cleveland, Ohio, at the 1899 convention of the Architectural League of America and published in the *Inland Architect and News Record* 33 (June 1899): 43. Reprinted in *The Testament of Stone: Themes of Idealism and Indignation from the Writings of Louis Sullivan.* Edited by Maurice English. Evanston: Northwestern University Press, 1963.

Kindergarten Chats. First published as a series in *Interstate Architect & Builder* 2–3 (16 February 1901–8 February 1902). Published in book form and edited by Claude F. Bragdon. Lawrence, Kansas: Fraternity Scarab Press, 1934.

"Suggestions in Artistic Brickwork." Foreword to a pamphlet entitled "Artistic Brick," published by the Hydraulic Press Brick Company, St. Louis, c. 1910. Reprinted in *The Prairie School Review* 4 (Second Quarter): 24–26.

"Development of Construction." *The Economist* 55 (24 June 1916): 1252; 56 (1 July 1916): 39–40.

Kindergarten Chats [revised 1918] and Other Writings. Edited by Isabella Athey. New York: Wittenborn, 1947.

A System of Architectural Ornament According with a Philosophy of Man's Powers. 1924. Reprinted. New York: The Eakins Press, 1967.

Autobiography of an Idea. 1924. Reprinted. New York: Dover, 1956.

General

Anscombe, Isabelle and Charlotte Gere. *Arts and Crafts in Britain and America.* London: Academy Editions, 1978.

Auction Catalogue of the Household Effects, Library, Oriental Rugs, Paintings, etc. of Mr. Louis Sullivan, the Well-Known Chicago Architect, November 29, 1909. Chicago: Williams, Barker and Severn Company, 1909. Burnham Library, The Art Institute of Chicago.

Bragdon, Claude F. "An American Architect: Being an Appreciation of Louis H. Sullivan," *House and Garden* 7 (January 1905): 47–55.

Brooks, H. Allen. *The Prairie School: Frank Lloyd Wright and His Midwest Contemporaries.* Toronto: University of Toronto Press, 1972.

Cathers, David M. *Furniture of the American Arts and Crafts Movement: Stickley and Roycroft Mission Oak.* New York: New American Library, 1981.

Darling, Sharon. *Chicago Ceramics and Glass: An Illustrated History, 1871 to 1933.* Chicago: Chicago Historical Society, 1979.

———. *Chicago Furniture: 1833–1983.* Chicago: Chicago Historical Society, 1984. Exhibition catalogue.

Gebhard, David. "William Gray Purcell and George Grant Elmslie and the Early Progressive Movement in American Architecture from 1900 to 1920." Ph.D. Dissertation, University of Minnesota, 1957.

Hanks, David. "Louis J. Millet and the Art Institute of Chicago." *Bulletin of the Art Institute of Chicago* 67 (March–April 1973): 13–19.

Hoffmann, Donald L. "The Brief Career of a Sullivan Apprentice: Parker N. Berry." *The Prairie School Review* 4 (First Quarter 1967): 7–15.

Lathrop, Alan K. "The Prairie School Bank: Patron and Architect." In *Prairie School Architecture in Minnesota, Iowa, Wisconsin.* St. Paul: Minnesota Museum of Art, 1982. Exhibition Catalogue.

"Louis Sullivan, 'The First American Architect'." *Current Literature* 52 (June 1912): 703–707.

Paul, Sherman, *Louis Sullivan: An Architect in American Thought.* Englewood Cliffs: Prentice-Hall, 1962.

"Recent Bank Buildings of the United States." *Architectural Record* 25 (January 1909): 1–55.

Reinhart, Martin W. "Norwegian-born Sculptor, Kristian Schneider: His Essential Contribution to the Development of Louis Sullivan's Ornamental Style." Paper presented to The Norwegian American Life of Chicago Symposium, 23 October 1982. Department of Architecture, The Art Institute of Chicago. Typescript.

Rucker, Darnell. *The Chicago Pragmatists.* Minneapolis: University of Minnesota Press, 1969.

Severens, Kenneth W. "The Reunion of Louis Sullivan and Frank Lloyd Wright." *The Prairie School Review* 12 (Third Quarter 1975): 5–22.

Sprague, Paul E. "The Architectural Ornament of Louis Sullivan and his Chief Draftsmen." Ph.D. Dissertation, Princeton University, 1969.

———. *The Drawings of Louis Henry Sullivan: A Catalogue of the Frank Lloyd Wright Collection at the Avery Architectural Library.* Princeton: Princeton University Press, 1979.

Vinci, John. *The Art Institute of Chicago: The Stock Exchange Trading Room.* Chicago: The Art Institute of Chicago, 1977.

"The Works of Sullivan an Inspiration Rather than a Model." *Western Architect* 23 (February 1916): 1.

Weingarden, Lauren S. "The Colors of Nature: Sullivan's Polychromy and 19th-Century Color Theory." *Winterthur Portfolio* 20 (Winter 1985): 243–260.

Individual Banks

National Farmers' Bank

Bennett, Carl K. "A Bank Built For Farmers," *The Craftsman* 15 (November 1908): 176–185.

Bowers, David P. "The National Farmers' Bank of Owatonna: A Documentation Project for the Northwestern Bank of Owatonna." Northwestern Bank, Owatonna, MN. Typescript.

Gebhard, David. "Louis Sullivan and George Grant Elmslie." *Journal of the Society of Architectural Historians* 19 (May 1960): 66–68.

———. "Letter to the Editor." *Prairie School Review* 4 (Third Quarter 1967): 34–35.

Millet, Louis J. "The National Farmers' Bank of Owatonna, Minn." *Architectural Record* 24 (October 1908): 248–255.

"Recent Bank Buildings of the United States." *Architectural Record* 25 (January 1909): 1–55.

Sprague, Paul E. "The National Farmers' Bank, Owatonna, Minnesota." *The Prairie School Review* 4 (Second Quarter 1967): 5–21.

Warn, Robert R. "Bennett & Sullivan, Client and Creator," *The Prairie School Review* 10 (Third Quarter 1973): 5–15.

———. "Louis H. Sullivan, '. . . an air of finality.' " *The Prairie School Review* 10 (Fourth Quarter): 5–19.

Peoples Savings Bank

Sullivan, Louis H. "Lighting the Peoples Savings Bank," *Illuminating Engineer* 6 (February 1912): 635.

Schuyler, Montgomery. "The Peoples Savings Bank." *The Architectural Record* 31 (January 1912): 44–56.

Welsh, Ted J. *The Peoples Bank: The First 75 Years.* Cedar Rapids: Peoples Bank and Trust Company, 1975. Privately printed and bound.

Land and Loan Office

Rebori, A. N. "The Architecture of Democracy: Three Recent Examples of the Work of Louis Sullivan." *Architectural Record* 39 (May 1916): 436–465.

Merchants National Bank

Rebori, A. N. "The Architecture of Democracy: Three Recent Examples of the Work of Louis Sullivan." *Architectural Record* 39 (May 1916): 436–465.

Severens, Kenneth W. "Louis Sullivan Builds a Small Town Bank." *AIA Journal* 65 (May 1976): 68–71.

Home Building Association

Rebori, A. N. "The Architecture of Democracy: Three Recent Examples of the Work of Louis Sullivan." *Architectural Record* 39 (May 1916): 436–465.

Peoples Savings and Loan Association

"Historical Sketches of Peoples Federal Savings and Loan Association." Brochure. Privately printed, [n.d.].

Tallmadge, Thomas. "The Peoples Savings and Loan Association Building of Sidney, Ohio," *The American Architect* 114 (25 October 1918): 480.

Farmers and Merchants Union Bank

"Farmers & Merchants Union Bank 100th Anniversary Edition: 1861–1961." *The Columbus Journal-Republic* (31 August 1961).

Tallmadge, Thomas. "The Farmers' and Merchants' Bank of Columbus, Wisconsin." *The Western Architect* 29 (July 1920): 63–65.